'erse

D0469187

# Grass Roots:
# The Universe
# of Home

Also by Paul Gruchow

*Journal of a Prairie Year*
*The Necessity of Empty Places*
*Minnesota: Images of Home*
*Travels in Canoe Country*

# Grass Roots:
## The Universe of Home

*Paul Gruchow*

MILKWEED
EDITIONS

Published 1995 by Milkweed Editions
Printed in the United States of America
Chapter head drawings by Carlyn Iverson.
Book design by Will Powers. The text of this book is set in
Baskerville.
Cover design by Adrian Morgan.
Cover photo by Michael Melford, Inc.
Endsheet photo by Beth Olson.
06  07  08  09  10     5  4
*First Edition*

Milkweed Editions is a not-for-profit publisher. We gratefully
acknowledge support from the Bush Foundation; the Target
Stores, Dayton's and Mervyn's by the Dayton Hudson Foundation;
Ecolab Foundation; General Mills Foundation; Honeywell
Foundation; Jerome Foundation; John S. and James L. Knight
Foundation; The McKnight Foundation; Andrew W. Mellon
Foundation; Minnesota State Arts Board through an appropria-
tion by the Minnesota State Legislature; Musser Fund; Challenge
and Literature Programs of the National Endowment for the Arts;
I. A. O'Shaughnessy Foundation; Piper Jaffray Companies, Inc.;
John and Beverly Rollwagen Fund of the Minneapolis Foundation;
The St. Paul Companies, Inc.; Star Tribune/Cowles Media
Foundation; Surdna Foundation; James R. Thorpe Foundation;
Lila Wallace-Reader's Digest Literary Publishers Marketing
Development Program, funded through a grant to the Council
of Literary Magazines and Presses; and generous individuals.

Library of Congress Cataloging-in-Publication Data

Gruchow, Paul.
    Grass roots : the universe of home / Paul Gruchow
       p.   cm.
    ISBN 1-57131-207-2
    1. Farm life—Minnesota.   2. Minnesota—Social life and
customs.   3. Gruchow, Paul.   4. Natural history—United
States.   I. Title
S521.5.M6G78   1995
635'.092—dc20                                        95–11006
    [B]                                                  CIP

For Bob Artley, who has lived what I believe.

*Acknowledgements*

I am grateful to Bill Holm, whose intervention persuaded
me to persevere in an effort I had decided to abandon;
to Emilie Buchwald—without whom this would have
been a much crankier book—for her superb skills as an
editor; to Elizabeth Umphrey, Richard Hamlow, and
Carol Bly for helpful readings of the book in manuscript;
to the staffs and members of The Land Institute, The
Land Stewardship Project, and the Minnesota Food
Association, who helped in many ways to give my ideas
shape and substance; and to the institutions that offered
me opportunities to try out these ideas as lectures or talks.

# Grass Roots:
# The Universe of Home

Grass Roots:
The Universe
of Home

**1**

# Home Is
a Place
in Time

W HAT IF ONE'S LIFE were not a
commodity, not something to
be bartered to the highest bidder,
or made to order? What if one's
life were governed by needs more
fundamental than acceptance or
admiration? What if one were simply to
stay home and plant some manner of garden?

To plant a garden is to enter the continuum of time.
Each seed carries in its genome the history that will pro-
pel it into the future, and in planting it we stretch one of
the long threads of our culture into tomorrow.

A home, like a garden, exists as much in time as in space. A home is the place in the present where one's past and one's future come together, the crossroads between history and heaven. I learned this truth the day we buried my mother.

In the previous month, I had felt often like a man without an anchor. We were living in St. Paul and expecting our first child. For my wife it was a difficult and somewhat dangerous pregnancy. Christmas passed and the days turned toward the new year. The baby was overdue. In those same days, Mother was lying in a hospital bed in Montevideo, Minnesota, emaciated and in pain. She had already lost a brave battle against cancer but was unwilling, just yet, to concede defeat, for reasons that were, to me, mysterious. She was long past delusion about her prospects. My own heart resided in both places, full of fear and hope at the same time. I did not know where my body should be.

On the penultimate day of the old year, the baby, after a stubborn resistance of her own, finally came. She was big and beautiful and healthy. She gave one lusty cry as she entered the world and then lay quietly while she was bathed and dressed, looking about the room in wide-eyed wonder.

I telephoned Mother with the news. She said with surprising energy that she hoped she might see the baby before she died. But that day a fierce cold front had settled over Minnesota. For more than a week daytime temperatures did not rise above zero. We were, as I suppose first-time parents always are, terrified of our responsibilities. The baby seemed so helpless and fragile. We did not dare risk the three-hour drive to the hospital.

One cloudy morning in mid-January the weather at last broke. We bundled up the baby and made a dash for

Montevideo. In the darkened hospital room, we intro-
duced grandmother and granddaughter. The baby slept
against the rails of the bed while Mother fondled her
with eyes too small for their bony sockets. They joined
hands, the baby's soft, fat, and warm, Mother's cold,
gaunt, and hard. With tremendous effort, Mother whis-
pered three words barely audible above the hum of the
humidifier.

"Is she healthy?" she asked. We wept, because she was.

When we arrived back home, the telephone was
ringing. A nurse was on the line with the word, hardly
news, that Mother had died.

The weather was still bitter and gray the day we
buried her in the little cemetery at St. John's Lutheran
Church. After the ceremony the three children—Kathy,
Paulette, and I—who felt strangely like children again
that day, vulnerable and bewildered in an impossibly big
world, took refuge one last time in the farmhouse where
we had laughed and cried, together and alone, so many
times.

We had meant to see to the household goods. There
would not be many other opportunities for it; we lived at
a distance from one another and seldom found ourselves
together. But almost the first items we came across were
the photo albums.

We sat in the living room then, not bothering to
light the lamp, looking at the pictures and talking until
the day died.

"Do you remember when Mother turned toward
the back seat of the car and said, 'Where's your sister?'
and Paul said, 'Oh, she fell out a long time ago,' and
she *had*?"

"Do you remember the day Mother told the
neighbor she couldn't go to the Women's Christian

Temperance Union meeting because her wine was ready for bottling?"

"Do you remember the day Kathy fell through the outhouse hole?"

"Do you remember the day you rode your bicycle down the driveway with no hands and it made me so mad I stomped the spokes out of my bicycle's wheels?"

"Do you remember the time we floated a pound of butter in Mother's hot laundry starch?"

Do you remember?

Do you remember?

The stories tumbled as if out of an overstuffed closet. Sometimes we had three of them going at once. We laughed until we ached. I remember it now as one of the happiest afternoons of my life, the metamorphosis of a friendship deepening as the years pass and we three face our own mortalities. I think that I have never been more exactly at home, more tenaciously alive, than that afternoon, when old joy and new sorrow and present love reverberated together inside me.

All history is ultimately local and personal. To tell what we remember, and to keep on telling it, is to keep the past alive in the present. Should we not do so, we could not know, in the deepest sense, how to inhabit a place. To inhabit a place means literally to have made it a habit, to have made it the custom and ordinary practice of our lives, to have learned how to wear a place like a familiar garment, like the garments of sanctity that nuns once wore. The word habit, in its now-dim original form, meant *to own*. We own places not because we possess the deeds to them, but because they have entered the continuum of our lives. What is strange to us—unfamiliar—can never be home.

It is the fashion just now to disparage nostalgia.

Nostalgia, we believe, is a cheap emotion. But we forget what it means. In its Greek roots it means, literally, the return to home. It came into currency as a medical word in nineteenth-century Germany to describe the failure to thrive of the displaced persons, including my own ancestors, who had crowded into that country from the east. Nostalgia is the clinical term for homesickness, for the desire to be rooted in a place — to know clearly, that is, what time it is. This desire need not imply the impulse to turn back the clock, which of course we cannot do. It recognizes, rather, the truth — if home is a place in time — that we cannot know where we are now unless we can remember where we have come from. The real romantics are those who believe that history is the story of the triumphal march of progress, that change is indiscriminately for the better. Those who would de-mythologize the past seem to forget that we also construct the present as a myth, that there is nothing in the wide universe so vast as our own ignorance. Knowing that is our one real hope.

# Rosewood Township

Paul DeWayne Gruchow,
Ed Will's Farm, Section 28,
Rosewood Township, Chippewa
County, Minnesota, USA, North
America, Western Hemisphere,
Earth, Milky Way, Universe. I
wrote the words over and over in my best
Palmer-method penmanship, arranging them like the
lines of a poem. For me they held a terrible fascination.
I felt about them as I did one Sunday morning when the
preacher pronounced the words, "As far as the east is
from the west," a phrase so magnificent and expansive,

so unfathomable, that it caused me to shudder.
Rosewood Township was too small and out of the
way ever to be so parochial as some great capital. Its
people never imagined that they were being watched or
admired from afar. In a billion years it would not have
occurred to anyone in Rosewood Township to refer to it
as The Big Apple. There were people who were born
in Rosewood Township and never intended to leave,
who desired to live nowhere else and perhaps had no
curiosity about doing so. But even the most optimistic
inhabitant of Rosewood Township understood its signifi-
cance to be obscure, limited mainly to the astonishing
connections that might be drawn between it and every
corner of the universe.

As a reminder, as a talisman, perhaps as an incan-
tation, I wrote those words on the inside cover of every
Big Chief tablet I carried to school: Paul DeWayne
Gruchow, Ed Will's farm, Section 28, Rosewood Township,
Chippewa County, Minnesota, USA, Western Hemi-
sphere, Earth, Milky Way, Universe.

Ed Will owned our farm and operated it until his retirement. I have been told how infatuated we children were
with him, how we would follow him everywhere when he
came to visit, peppering him with questions that always
began with his name. *Ed Will, how long are you going to
stay? Ed Will, did you bring us any pennies?* (He always
had.) *Ed Will, where do rabbits sleep? Ed Will, can snails
sing?* But I remember almost nothing about him. I think
of him as big and brisk, but I knew him when every adult
seemed huge and was able to outstride my short legs. He
wore a town man's straw hat, not a farmer's cap, and
gray-striped overalls, not the more practical blue ones
that my father and I wore. One time we visited him after

he had gone to a nursing home. Father and Mother went up to his room while we children waited on the porch, where half a dozen old men were slumped in wheel- chairs. One of them suddenly let out a tremendous bellow, a nurse came running with a long-necked urinal, and he peed into it while my sister and I stared, more in awe of his grand indifference to us than of anything else.

When I was eight or nine, I stole a book of matches, which I had been strictly forbidden to have. As I was lighting them in the hayloft of Ed Will's barn, I dropped one, still burning, into the loose hay that filled the loft and could not retrieve it. The place exploded. By the time I reached the stairs, the interior of the loft raged with a searing light. The flames were already piercing the roof as I escaped through a main-floor door. I ran frantically to the pump, drew a single pail of water, and threw it at the barn, recognizing the futility of the ges- ture even as I carried it out. Then I ran hysterically toward the house, crying, "The barn is on fire! The barn is on fire!"

Neighbors and passersby, drawn by the smoke that mushroomed above us like a bomb cloud, formed a bucket brigade and kept the roof of the house wet, sav- ing it, but every other building on the place was by nightfall either destroyed or damaged. The animals in the pasture, smelling the smoke, panicked and fled into the barn for safety. Not one of them, not even the cat, survived. Grain, tools, and machinery were destroyed. The embers smoldered for a week. The bitter smell of charred flesh lingered even longer.

I was out of my mind with grief and fear. I imagined being sent to prison. I had, young as I was, a faint sense of what my carelessness would mean to a family already dangling by an economic thread. The smell of smoke and burned flesh nauseated me. I took to my loft and could not speak or eat for days. Ten years passed before I found the courage to talk about that afternoon.

The fire inspector came a few days later. I cowered in the house while my father went out, as he had said he must, to tell the official and Ed Will that his son had accidentally started the blaze. I could not hear the long, murmured conversation from the little window of my loft. When a story appeared in the local newspaper a couple of days later, it reported that the inspector had determined that the fire had been set off by spontaneous combustion. A few days later, Ed Will visited the farm again. He was not a wealthy man, and he was getting old; he would not rebuild, he said.

He had two nickels in his pocket, one for my sister and one for me, and he gave us both big hugs.

The community in which I grew up was pious to a fault—I came to believe that piety ought to be counted among the deadly sins—but even there, rectitude, out of consideration for a child, sometimes gave way to compassion.

Ed Will's land was at the southeast corner of Section 28 of Rosewood Township. There were two eighty-acre plots, one running east and west from the southeast section corner, and the other running north and south through the middle of the section. They made an L in the classic shape of a farmhouse. One hundred sixty acres, a quarter of a square mile, was standard size for a farm in the early 1950s. Our east-west eighty was generally level, running slightly uphill at the east end. The north-south eighty was flat for a quarter of a mile and then dipped into a large cattail marsh, which was low enough that the farmstead could not be seen from it. The topsoil was rich black prairie loam, fertile

and generally friable, but with a tendency to harden
into something like concrete if worked when too wet.
My father rented this land on shares. He supplied
the tools, the labor, and the seeds and kept two-thirds of
the crop. Land in the early 1950s still passed mainly
from generation to generation, but my grandfather, the
son of Polish refugees, never owned land, and Ed Will's
children, if he had any, were not farmers. So we were
part of the underclass of tenant-farmers in the larger underclass of rural society, at a time when farmers still
thought of themselves as the salt of the earth but after
the Jeffersonian ideal of the yeoman farmer had lost
its savor.

Our farm was, if anything, less diverse than average.
We raised corn, wheat, oats, soybeans, and flax and kept
goats, sheep, and chickens, but many farms also had pigs
and beef or dairy cows, and, consequently, alfalfa and
more pasture than we did. My father was more interested
in horticulture than in livestock—he was a gardener at
heart—and sharecropping discouraged investments in
pasture and hay, which were not as advantageous to the
landowner.

A popular feature of our county weekly, the
*Montevideo American*, in those days was the Mystery Farm.
An aerial photograph of a farmstead was published,
readers competed to identify its occupants, and the first
reader with the correct answer won a small prize. A story
about the farm followed in the next edition. The stories
always included a paragraph about the farmer's conservation practices and described recent improvements to
the buildings. Many farm people were installing bathrooms at that time.

Reading through these stories not long ago, I was
struck by how diversified farming still was then, in what,

one realizes now, was the last stage of the industrialization of American farming. There does not appear to have been any farm that did not have four or five kinds of crops and two or three kinds of livestock. The average farm, too, was a quarter the size of one today, and the typical field was comparatively tiny—twenty-five acres of a crop was a big spread, and there were many fields of fewer than ten acres. I was struck as well by how much land was not under active cultivation. Often a quarter of the land on a farm is described as in pasture or is unaccounted for.

There were fencerows then. Corn hybrids were less sturdy than they are now, and genetic resistance to the corn borer was still to be developed, so there was more downed corn in the fields. Corn pickers were less efficient than today's combines, too. After the harvest, a lot of corn remained in the fields. The common practice was to turn the livestock loose in them to fatten on the gleanings, which required that fields be fenced. Fences hemmed in the plows. So every farm was ringed by a greenway, in which prairie grasses and flowers grew, mice nested, and ground squirrels, pocket gophers, and badgers burrowed, supporting populations of predators —foxes, skunks, weasels, feral cats, owls, hawks. The landscape was, in a modest way, still hospitable to wild as well as to domesticated life. My father had supplemented his income by trapping. Reading the old files of the *Montevideo American*, I understood how trapping was possible.

Such a contest as Mystery Farm had reader appeal in those days. There was a reliable chance that the occupants of the chosen farmstead could be identified, and that the people who lived in the buildings were, in fact, connected to the surrounding community. Farming and farm people, quite aside from this particular contest, were once big news in Montevideo, the seat of Chippewa County. The progress of the rains, the arrival of the corn borers, the annual egg show, the annual meeting of the rural power cooperative (which drew more than 3,000 participants), the corn-picking contest, the yields at harvest time: all these were front-page news in 1952, the year my family moved to Rosewood Township from a seven-acre vegetable and berry farm in an adjoining township. Social news from Rosewood Township commanded a weekly column in the *Montevideo American.* I read in it that we had Christmas Eve dinner that year with my grandmother, aunt and uncle, and cousins, and that after dinner we attended services at St. John's Lutheran Church. When the program was over, each child received a bag of treats, including an apple, some peanuts in the shell, chocolate stars, pillow-shaped peppermints, and ribbons of hard candy.

Chippewa County is among the most rural counties in the nation, one of the few where agriculture still accounts for at least half of the gross production. Farming remains central to the economics of Chippewa County, and it is all there is in Rosewood Township. But there aren't many farmers anymore — there are producers and marketers. Farming once entailed something more than production and marketing, more than a livelihood. It was a culture, a vocation. Vocational agriculture was a subject taught in high schools, but in my experience of it, there was a good deal of talk about pig rations and weed-eradication methods and none about farming as work with a moral or social purpose. A profound change took place when people stopped talking about agriculture and started talking about agribusiness — the death of the culture in agriculture.

Our farmstead was sheltered on the west and north by a grove of maples. There was a farmhouse and, next to it, a little summer kitchen, a place where the cooking could be done in hot weather without turning the house itself into a blast furnace. There were also, until the fire, a hip-roofed barn, a chicken house, a hog house, a machine shed, and a granary. The granary had two bins, one with slatted sides for corn and the other, across a covered alley, with solid walls for small grains. The barn enclosed a big hay loft and was fitted for dairy cows, although we didn't keep any. Next to the barn rose a windmill, still in working order when we lived there. One of Father's annual chores was to climb the windmill and grease the gears at the top.

The house had two main rooms downstairs, a living room and a bedroom. An enclosed porch served as kitchen and dining room. Up a steep staircase, snuggled beneath the attic crawl space, were two tiny slant-roofed rooms tall enough for a child to stand in, but not everywhere, and just barely. My twin sister and I occupied these rooms when we were old enough to leave the main bedroom. After our younger sister came along, I moved to the summer kitchen, which had neither insulation nor interior walls. One night I shared it with a skunk, visible in the moonlight, that padded about, sniffing and poking into every cranny and upsetting the wastebasket while I lay frozen in my bed. Climbing out from under the mountain of handmade quilts on winter mornings and getting dressed in a room where the temperature was below freezing, and sometimes below zero, was a stiff test of character. But I loved that place for the privacy and independence it afforded me. It was my Walden cabin; like Thoreau, I spent my nights alone, but a hot meal, laundry service, and companionship always waited in the house when I needed them.

The main house was sparsely furnished. It could hardly have been otherwise, given its minuscule size. The kitchen had a cupboard, a chrome dinette set of the kind fashionable in the 1950s, and a cookstove fueled with wood and corn cobs. A couch, two or three chairs, and an oil-burning stove that sat on a metal fire pad appointed the living room, as well as the only piece of art that I can remember, a rendering of the Last Supper in an oval metal frame painted gold. In the bedroom: a bed, a dresser, and a vanity table overhung with a big mirror, the only one in the house. You can estimate the economic status of a household by counting its mirrors. Upstairs: two beds, two dressers. The floors were covered in patterned linoleums, the walls in print wallpapers with ornamental borders; the whole place was a pastel panic of plaids, paisleys, and floral stripes.

Food was stored in a root cellar, a dugout with fieldstone walls and a floor that was muddy in the spring and dusty the rest of the year. It was reached through a trap door just to the right of the front door of the house. Dank and lit by a bare bulb, its walls were lined with shelves for the canned goods. Mother put up about 700 quarts of produce a year: fruits, vegetables, sauces, jams, jellies, pickles, fruit butters, krauts, meats. There were also a big bin in which the root vegetables were stored and tin canisters in which apples, wrapped individually in strips of newsprint, kept almost until spring.

In the springtime we children dreaded the trip to the root cellar. You might be told to run down there to fetch a pot of potatoes. This meant raising the trap door; descending into the dark through a curtain of spider webs that tangled in your hair and caught in your eyebrows; standing in the mud; and groping for the light

string, which, when pulled, made you feel better, although the bulb didn't, in fact, illuminate the potato
bin. You plunged your hand in, knowing that you could
find your fingers sinking into a rotten tuber, or that you
could scare up one of the tiger salamanders that had
wintered there in the warmth. It would scamper across
your bare toes, giving you the bejeebees. The only thing
worse was fetching eggs from under a temperamental
and sharp-beaked hen in the mood to brood.

Ours was largely a subsistence farm. The chickens,
when they were not molting, provided eggs. Occasionally
one of them submitted its neck to the chopping block
and, after a final headless romp around the yard, its
wings beating desperately, it would be scalded in boiling
water; its feathers would be plucked (the pin feathers
stuck in your fingers as if still begging for mercy); and it
would be boiled until tender, then panfried and served
with gravy, made from the drippings, and mashed potatoes. The onions in the pan came from our garden; the
flour to thicken the gravy was ground from wheat raised
on the farm; the goats made the milk; the potatoes, because we ate so many of them, were raised in their own
bed apart from the garden. To accompany the potatoes
and the chicken, there might be string beans, or peas, or
beets, grown also in the garden, or asparagus gleaned
from the fencerows; and with the bread there would be
strawberry jam, perhaps, or apple butter, or honey from
one of our own hives of bees. For dessert there might be,
in summer, a fresh-baked fruit pie, or, in winter, a sauce
—plum, or apple, or groundcherry. The salt, the butter,
and the sugar were bought in town. Breakfasts were also
imported: the menu was the same every day—oatmeal
with raisins and an orange or grapefruit. But what the
farm, and our own labors, could provide, they did; and it

is, I think, more than fancy that what we ate, because of this, had a special flavor and meaning.

The work went round and round: spring plowing, disking, planting, cultivating, the first hay harvest, canning, the small grain harvest, the second cutting of hay, soybeans out, corn out, cornstalks chopped, potato digging, fall plowing, wood cutting, butchering, boiling and dying traps, running the trap lines, skinning and stretching furs, corn shelling, lambing, until the rains quit, the puddles dried, and the trees bloomed—time again to start the spring plowing. It was classical work done mainly in the classical ways on a classical schedule. The weekly house schedule had the same regularity: Mondays, washing; Tuesdays, ironing; Wednesdays, baking; Thursdays, sewing, gardening, preserving; Fridays, town days; Saturdays, cleaning; Sundays, days of worship and rest.

To each day, and to each season, was dedicated a suitable labor, but no labor was ever exactly repeated. No year was ever the same as another, and each field had its own character. Farming the land was always new work, not repetitious but experimental, always unfolding, destined never to be completed. Sometimes the experiments worked; sometimes an idea that succeeded once, or ten times, failed on the next trial. Exactly why no one could say, since experiments on the farm are not like experiments in the laboratory, where the variables can be reduced to known elements. A subsistence farmer cannot afford the luxury of Cartesian thinking, but is obliged instead to work in the real world, the whole world, where one thing is indivisibly connected to another.

In the house the work was never quite the same work, either. Each batch of bread, for example, was the product of a freshly ground canister of wheat that was not industrially milled and therefore varied from year to year, from grinding to grinding, and a cake of yeast that constituted a community of living organisms that multiplied, or didn't, according to its own state of vigor; and each kneading was a new and individual kneading, conducted with reference to my mother's memory of the exact texture that, from this lump of dough, under these conditions of heat and humidity, considering the fecundity of this yeast and the character of this batch of flour, would solicit a fine loaf of bread. The loaf would be baked to perfection according to its color and to the sound it made when it was tapped, each fire having been built to the occasion, its heat depending upon the condition of the materials that fueled it and upon the circumstances under which it was stoked or banked, according to the judgment of the baker.

My father planted a field as my mother set out a batch of dough to rise, each paying attention to experience, employing techniques acquired through long practice, and varying the methods as present conditions or the impulse to experiment dictated, each relying upon the faith that these resources would meet the exigencies ahead but knowing that the fruit ultimately depended upon the season. The work was creative; it was like making a poem, or dancing, or saying a prayer.

For me, the most important place on the farm was the cattail marsh at its north end. To get there, you took the farm's interior road, a grass track that ran east to the edge of the maple grove and then north as far as the waterway that drained into the slough from the east. The physical distance was not quite half a mile, but so far as I was concerned it might have been halfway around the world.

Here was a piece of Rosewood Township as it had
existed for thousands of years, a surviving testament to
the tallgrass prairie, and the richest and most complex
representative of it. As measured by its biomass, a cattail
marsh is one of the earth's most productive features.
Only in a tropical rainforest does life reproduce more
extravagantly. Rosewood Township at settlement was a
great ocean of grass lapping across a level plain. It had
nothing that could properly be called a hill. The landscape rose and fell in swells and swales, like the sea. It
had no trees, no river or stream, no lake. Because the
moisture that fell had nowhere to go, it stayed on the
land. The tall grasses caught and held the snow against
the fierce winds in winter; in spring the thirsty sod
soaked up the meltwaters, and they trickled down
through the immeasurable miles of roots that constitute
the hidden jungle of a prairie and into the groundwater
basins and channels that are its unseen lakes and rivers.
The water that the ground could not absorb drained as
far as the nearest low place, creating marshes like the
one on our farm.

Most of these were not permanent bodies of water.
As summer wore on and the wet days of May gave way to
dusty August, the ponds evaporated, exposing ovals of
black mud, ringed by rank growths of cattails, rushes,
and tall wetland flowers. These ovals baked and cracked,
the rich alkaline deposits in them collecting as fine white
powder. But the marshes persisted long enough, most
years, to produce flocks of ducks and geese by the thousands, to shelter dozens of kinds of songbirds; and the
marsh waters were as thick as a primordial soup with
crustaceans, insect larvae, and with microorganisms
by the billions per teaspoonful. This profusion of
life attracted frogs, snakes, and insects numbering in

the thousands of species; and so came the skunks and weasels, the minks and foxes, the raccoons, the mice and shrews, and on the uplands the burrowing animals, the ground squirrels and badgers, and pocket gophers; and in pursuit of them came the wolves and coyotes, the raptors, the hawks and owls; and in the tall grasses around them grazed the great herbivores, the bison, elk, and antelope. At the edges of the large sloughs, such as ours, a few willows and cottonwoods took root, casting a rare shade upon the flowerful but severe landscape; and the water lasted from year to year, attracting muskrats and turtles, clams and crayfishes.

There were a million things to see in our marsh. I spent many days and whole nights there when I was a boy, trying to catch sight of them all. I could never succeed. It was a fabulous textbook to me, a storybook as fantastic as *Arabian Nights*. It was my university, my theater, my refuge and strength. When I rejoiced, I went there to celebrate; when I was sad, to be consoled. In every weather, I worshipped there.

I imagine that every child fantasizes an independent life, freed from the constraints and constrictions of youthfulness and of the household. My own dreams, when I was emerging from childhood into adolescence, centered on some version of living in the wild. I dreamed of being, sometimes in the company of one or another of my cousins, a kind of human coyote, a stealthy and wily opportunist, hiding out by day in groves or cornfields or in the drainage ditches that were such a prominent feature of the landscape I knew, emerging at twilight to hunt or fish or forage for food. I would be, I thought, a nomad, never lingering anywhere so long as to be found out, always living with undetectable lightness upon the land, a hermit, existing at the edges of society but outside of it and unknown to it.

Or I would be a trapper living in a remote northern forest. Because the trapping I knew took place in the late fall and early winter, the world I inhabited in this dream was always wintery. There was a snug log cabin at the center of it. A pair of snowshoes and several pelts on wire stretchers hung on the cabin wall beside the door. Inside, a fire blazed in an open fireplace. A stew bubbled in a cast-iron pot above the flames. I would go out in the springtime, my furs loading down my canoe, to a settlement to trade my catch for another year's supplies, and without stopping even for a night, I would turn right around and head back to my snug house in the woods. I dreamed of living where it was wild, but also of living outside of a money economy. I never dreamed of wealth.

My mother, I think, would have preferred a more social life. She loved to talk; she struck up conversations easily with strangers. One day in the laundromat in town, when the news was of an escapee from the county jail, she discoursed at great length to a stranger on the utter incompetency of the local sheriff. "Why, that man couldn't find his head if it wasn't fastened on," she concluded. The stranger excused himself politely and left the premises. There was a long silence in the laundromat, punctuated by the slap of buttons against the insides of dryers.

Finally another woman in the place spoke. "Do you know who that was?" she asked my mother.

"Haven't the faintest idea," Mother said.

"That was the sheriff."

Mother laughed loudly. "Well, at least I didn't tell him any lies," she said.

After my father died, she took up ballroom dancing.

She had grown up in a household kept by Norwegian immigrants with a strong sense of propriety, first cousins bound in what may have been a marriage of convenience. Mother's parents had adopted her from an unwed Irish girl in St. Louis. At eighteen she married my father, a Polish farm boy, bright but uneducated, a convert as a teenager to a dour Christian fundamentalism of his own making, but worst of all, poor—entirely unacceptable to Norwegian in-laws with social ambitions. My parents had an affectionate marriage, but one in which most forms of public pleasure, especially dancing, were forbidden. By the time my mother was nineteen she had twin babies, her rich and beautiful hair had thinned and turned mousy from the strain of childbirth, and she was living, in the aftermath of World War II, in a twenty-four-foot square cinder block basement with a flat, ground-level tar paper roof and no windows, electricity, or plumbing. So when the opportunity came, in her forties, to dance, she seized upon it extravagantly. For all I know, she even had a drink now and then. One day I drove her home from the hospital. She had undergone a radical mastectomy and was still weak and woozy, but she insisted she'd be just fine. When I called the next day to see how she was doing, she was in high spirits. She had been out dancing until three that morning. "I guess your old mother isn't dead yet!" she said. She had some kind of economic longing, too, for richer fare; for the last year of her life, until her body rejected food, and although there was a day, a neighbor recently told me, when she was down to her last stick of wood for the furnace, she ate a steak for dinner every night.

She laughed a lot, especially at her own jokes, always a bit too boisterously. I do the same, and so did my grandmother on my father's side. My grandmother laughed with pleasure, but she also laughed whenever anything went wrong. The more dire the news, the harder she laughed, not that she thought travesty funny, but because she had a heavy sense of fate. When things went wrong, what else could you do? You could never tell, when my grandmother laughed, whether she was amused or unbearably sad. I am the same way. When I laugh, I hear the loud, ambiguous laughter of my mother and grandmother.

My father would have liked, I think, a life of greater adventure. He was the youngest of the five children in his family who lived past infancy, and the only male. His ancestors were Polish farmers, early followers of the Reformation who fled oppression in their own country, first settling around Berlin and then emigrating to the United States. My grandparents grew up in the rich farming country of northwest Iowa, too late to home-stead; later in his life, because of an inheritance of my mother's, my father became the first Gruchow in his di-rect line to own land. Grandfather, as was the peasant custom, dutifully served his own father until his twenty-first birthday; on that morning, he married a German girl who did laundry for the wealthy folks who sum-mered in the Iowa Great Lakes. On the afternoon of their wedding day, grandfather put up a load of hay while grandmother went off to do a load of wash. Perhaps they were shivareed that evening by friends and neighbors, but a honeymoon was out of the ques-tion. Eventually they migrated from Iowa to much poorer land in Minnesota, where they lived out their days as farmers on shares. In retirement, grandfather kept a few chickens and watched television; grand-mother rubbered on the party telephone line, kept track of the comings and goings of the neighbors, and read children's books, the only kind she could read. They were, I would say, happy; at least they never wanted or expected any other kind of life.

Although my father was a gifted student, he left school after the eighth grade to work, and he, like his father, worked at home without pay until he was twenty-one, when he married my mother, whom he had met at a roller skating rink. The couple settled in the neighborhood where they had been raised. There they remained for the rest of their lives, venturing beyond it, so far as I can recall, except for an occasional Sunday afternoon picnic, only five or six times: a honeymoon trip to the Black Hills, a trip one winter to New Orleans, a blueberrying venture in northern Minnesota, one or two trips to the state fair in St. Paul, and one to Minneapolis to attend my own wedding. My father owned two suits in his lifetime, the dapper double-breasted navy one he was married in and the gray polyester one he was buried in, and four cars, a Model A Ford, a Chevrolet, and two Studebakers. The last of the Studebakers, a pink Lark, stout and gaudy, was, I believe, the single material indulgence of his life. He gave something close to half the family income, after farm expenses, to the church. He had a keen awareness of the many people in the world who were less fortunate than he. This was not a decision about which the rest of the family was consulted, or one in which they would likely have concurred.

My father's dreams were centered on lost worlds. He was a romantic, not in the perverted sense in which the word is now customarily used — fanciful, impractical, unrealistic — but in the older sense: he was an idealist, attracted to the idea — so far from his own life — of adventure, a celebrant of nature, of the ordinary person, of freedom of spirit. To use the label "romantic" to dismiss any idea currently out of fashion also means to condemn it for its devotion to principle rather than expediency, to ordinary human beings rather than to those who would exploit them, and to freedom from intellectual tyranny. I, like my father, am, in the old sense, romantic; I do not believe that idealism is a delusion.

The lost world of Atlantis fascinated my father. In this I suppose he was under the influence of Ignatius Donnelly, Minnesota's great agrarian rabble-rouser and sometimes crackpot scholar. So did the story of the Arcadians; his was the romance of pastoral peacefulness and simplicity. One still meets people like him in the countryside, people who have been to the city only once and thought that was one time too many, who feel awkward even in the big rural county seat towns, who abhor crowds, bustle, and fanciness, who might enjoy racing stock cars at county speedways on the weekends but are discombobulated by the aggressive swirl of traffic on urban free-for-all-ways — people perfectly content to be who they are and where they are. One also meets the same kind of person in cities, sometimes in high places, the sort of person who went to the countryside once for a weekend and thought to die of boredom, who shudders to imagine the cloying, stultifying, shabby meanness of life in the kind of hamlet where the only restaurant serves beef commercials and there isn't a good show or nightclub or store that sells a shirt not made in Taiwan in a hundred miles. The only difference between the two, really, is that one kind of person is thought to be a bumpkin, a hayseed, a hick, and the other is regarded as a sophisticate. What divides them, mainly, is not so much who they are as what they have.

My father was also inspired by the Cajuns, by the story of their lonely wanderings in search of a place to

live in peace, until at last they came to the bayous of
Louisiana, a swampy land, teeming with snakes and alligators and mosquitoes, that nobody else wanted, and of
how they made there a vibrant culture suitable to the
place. Our solitary family trip out of state, to Louisiana,
was, I now understand, a kind of pilgrimage. It is fashionable at the moment to reread this continent's settlement
history as a morality tale: the venal avarice of the con-
quering horde. One such account that I happen to have
on my desk describes "the European predilection to kill
first and ask questions later." I doubt that this characterizes the average settler, who was, I think, an Old World
failure in search not of a new world to conquer but of a
refuge, a place with a few cows, a garden, a house of
one's own, as far away from trouble as possible. The
worst kind of sentimentality supposes that bad results
generally flow from bad intentions. Often, our best intentions are the ones that confound us.

The refuge my father dreamed of was in Alaska,
where it was still possible to homestead. *Alaska* magazine
was the only one he ever subscribed to. My father often,
as if it were an icon, displayed a photograph, gleaned
from the magazine, of some huge cabbages growing in
the Sitka Valley. He held them in the kind of regard that
an art connoisseur might have for a rare oil by an Old
Master. The place was, to him, never merely Alaska, but
The Land of the Midnight Sun, where a person could
live free and unencumbered, simply, off the land. As a
practical matter, living off the land required a natural system still more or less intact. My father did not want to
conquer the land, to build an empire, or to leave any
legacy other than his example. He mocked the back-to-
the-land hippies of my own generation, but not because
he had any fundamental disagreement with their

dreams; it was their ineptness that bothered him. He, too, was a dreamer, but a dreamer who could build a house, fashion a tool out of scrap metal, prune an apple tree, shear a sheep, and hive a swarm of honey bees.

I was, I think, ten the afternoon I decided to act out my own dream. Mother was at a Ladies Aid meeting; I had only recently been released from the humiliation of having to accompany her. Dad was in the field. I gathered the quilt and pillow from my bed, stole a quart of dill pickles from the cellar, cut a cabbage and pulled some carrots from the garden and piled these onto the quilt, added a box of matches, an empty tin can, a length of fishing line, and a hook and bobber, gathered the ends of the blanket up into a bundle, and set off down the field road toward the slough.

The road, about a third of a mile long, skirted the plum thicket on the edge of the farmstead grove and then turned north along the property line toward the cattail marsh. The plums were still green, but there were a few ripe wild grapes, tart, mostly seeds and skin, as refreshing as lemonade. I picked a bunch, tucked them into my bundle, and trudged on down the lane, two narrow dirt tracks with a growth of weeds—plaintain, foxtail, pigeon grass—between. On both sides of the track towered rows of corn tall enough to hide a man, their ears just at the milk stage. I plucked foxtail stems as I walked and chewed on their sweet, succulent ends.

The field was level, good black prairie loam soil, all the way to the slight ridge that, even in winter, hid the marsh from view. Over the ridge, the land made a shallow basin, longer than wide, running northeast to southwest and draining at its southwestern end, when the water was high, into a tile; the slightly lower basin on the neighbor's land had already been drained. Ours hadn't, I think, because Ed Will was too old to be interested in new capital investments.

The slough was oval; its shape was accentuated by the concentric rings of vegetation that defined it: row crops on the uplands; then a gray-green ring dominated by the weedier prairie plants: common milkweeds, goldenrods, sunflowers, prairie dock; in the dampest soils and shallowest waters, a few swamp milkweeds, cup plants, Joe Pye weeds; then the thickets of cattails and hidden among them the houses and hidden waterways of muskrats; and then the gray-blue, irregular oval of open water at the center of the marsh, which lasted into August only in the wet years. In the dry ones, the water evaporated away, the water plants shriveled up, and a lacy network of deep cracks, like the surface of an old china plate, opened in the marsh bottom, which had an ashen glaze of alkaline precipitates. In the driest years, one could go walking on the marsh bottom, stepping over its dark cracks, the shells of pond snails and the brown tubers of cattails crunching underfoot, a sound as arid as the landscape itself.

At the upper end of the pond, there was a woodpile, the remains of a big old cottonwood tree that had once grown there, in which I had trapped both a weasel and a skunk. Perhaps now in the August heat it sheltered a snake. I would have to go there later to investigate. But for the moment I was content to spread my quilt beneath the other cottonwood tree, the one still standing at the lower end of the pond, just beyond a small thicket of willows. I loved it for its ragged heights. As I lay there gazing up into the sky, it sometimes looked as if the tree would snag one of the cottonball clouds of prairie summer, so that I might, at last, climb up and get the feel of a cloud. I loved the cottonwood for its thickly textured bark, as

brown and furrowed as my grandfather's hands. I loved it
for its heart-shaped leaves, clattering in the breeze on
their petioles, making a sound like gentle summer rain. I
loved it for its shade, the thin, dappled shade of a solitary
tree, which admitted the sun in yellow patches, as
through the panes of a window into an empty room on a
quiet afternoon. It was the light and shade of close summer afternoons, slightly moist, warm as a blanket, lazy,
accompanied in the background by the okaleeing of
blackbirds and the musty smell of marshwater and the
feel of damp earth between bare toes.

There was nothing better to do on such an afternoon in the shade of such a tree than nothing: the illicit
sweetness of idleness when there was, as always, work that
needed doing, work that would have to wait. Nothing to
do instead but to wait and watch, to listen, to doze, to
dream, to pluck apart the petals of a flower, to spy on
leafhoppers and spittle bugs, to host a tree frog in the
palm of a hand, to imitate the droning of a bumblebee,
to anticipate the fall of a green leaf. Donald Hall reports,
in *Life Work,* the meaning of happiness, as it was reported
to him by an Indian acquaintance: *absorbedness.* I know, as
much from boyhood afternoons at the marsh as from
anything, what he meant: those brief moments in life
when one is so occupied as to forget time, when time has
become a translucent pair of wings.

I prided myself on my ability to tell the time by the
sun. When I saw that it was after five o'clock, I made a
meal: a wedge of the cabbage, a couple of the carrots,
several dill pickles. I intended to forage for food and to
try my hand at cookery, but these were efforts that might
be made later, when I had settled in. The garden food, in
any case, ought to be eaten while it was still fresh. I
would have liked a glass of Kool Aid, I had to admit. The

meal was good and satisfying; if only I had thought to
bring a tomato, too. Our garden flourished in an old
pasture rich with the residue of animals. We gardened
organically, and many of the seeds we planted were, we
would say now, heirlooms, saved from the best plants of
previous seasons, the ones prized for their vigor and for
the intense flavor of their fruits. They were the end
product of generations of discriminating selection. The
sort of gardener I knew when I was growing up was a
small-time plant breeder and, although the cooking was
generally plain, an epicure: someone who judged a vegetable more by its taste than by its appearance. Our
everyday kitchens were supplied, as I was for my pur-
loined repast, with ingredients so fine that money could
not buy them. Possessing such richness was one of the
ways in which we were, although impecunious, rich.

After the meal, I climbed into the cottonwood tree,
took a lofty seat with a view of the marsh, and settled in
for the evening show. It was a show without much of a
plot, although I never tired of it. The shadows length-
ened; the light assumed a late, golden radiance; mama
ducks took a turn around the pond with their cheeping
chicks in tow; muskrats swam here and there, submerged
except for the upper third of their heads, making brown
arrows in the water from which their wakes spread like
feathery tails; the evening showed its colors; twilight rose,
as if out of the water, and spread like fog; the birds fell
silent; the first stars came out; the crickets began to
fiddle; and then there was the moon, its soft blue light
floating upon the darkness of the submerged earth or
held aloft upon the shimmering ostinato of the crickets,
a sound that accentuated the silence.

I began to feel sorry for myself as the night and the
silence deepened. Nobody had come looking for me.

Did this mean that I was not missed? Had no effort been made to find me? Perhaps days would pass before anybody noticed that I was not present. There would be some chore and nobody to do it, I supposed, and then somebody would finally look around and say, "You know, I haven't seen Paul lately, have you?"

"Now that you mention it, I don't think so."

"He always was one to disappear when there was work to do."

I, in the meantime, would be dead, drowned in the muck of the pond or struck by lightning in a passing thunderstorm, already bloated and starting to smell. There would be flies crawling in the sockets where my eyes had been. When they found me in that condition, they'd be sorry. Then there'd be a few tears for poor old unmissed Paul.

I was a little teary myself as I climbed down from the tree and wrapped myself in the quilt. My mother had made it of old flannel shirts and pajamas and worn-out overalls. There were twenty years of family history in that patchwork blanket, which had been mine for as long as I could remember. It felt good to be embraced in it now and to lay my head on a familiar pillow. I removed my eyeglasses and put them in the tin can for safekeeping. The bright drawbridge of the Milky Way dissolved into a vague glow. In a distant farmyard a dog barked.

I awoke in the dark hour just before dawn when the rabbits have come out to feed in the dewy grass, the owls are settling into their daytime roosts, and the songbirds have stirred and one at a time begun to sing, the hour of the day, in one strand of Native-American mythology, when all creatures sing to encourage the plants to drink the dew.

Nothing compelled me to rise from my bed beneath the cottonwood tree, and for a long time I didn't.

That was the first of hundreds of mornings that I have spent in out-of-the-way places, listening and watching as the dawn opens the day. When I arise in my house, brew a pot of coffee, read the morning newspapers, and go to my study to begin the day's work, I have submitted myself, usually pleasantly and productively, to the discipline of the clock. But there are other ways to follow time. One alternative is not to live hour by hour but moment by moment, understanding that a moment might last indeterminately, to live, that is, from experience to experience, as I do, perhaps instinctively, when I travel into nature. Dawn is one of the moments of this kind of time.

I had more practical considerations on my mind when I finally did get up. I needed to think about shelter. What would I do when it rained? When winter came? I walked around to the other end of the marsh to inspect the woodpile. Perhaps its pieces might be rearranged into some kind of hut. But that, I soon saw, was unlikely. I thought of a dugout such as the first white settlers in this country made, but the slopes in the vicinity of the marsh were gentle, the digging that would be required formidable, there was no prairie turf left with which to sod it, and I had neither a shovel nor the materials for making one. I could raise a teepee, but where would I find the skins, and how would I tan and sew them? The most logical solution, I thought, was to make a wigwam. The willows might be cut and bent to shape, and there were plenty of cattails from which mats for thatching might be fashioned. I cut an armful of cattail leaves, hauled them to my shelter beneath the cottonwood, and set to work. But the leaves were not as pliable as one would have thought—they had a tendency to crease when they were bent too far—and when I had assembled a whole mat it was not clear to me how to bind it. In any case, it hardly looked waterproof; either there was a better way to do the weaving or one would need to make a daunting number of mats and layer them. I wasn't prepared for these technical difficulties. Fortunately, rain did not seem imminent, and winter was months away.

In the books I particularly admired at this stage of my life—*Robinson Crusoe, The Swiss Family Robinson, Huckleberry Finn*—such difficulties never seemed to emerge. The people who got shipwrecked on islands or floated away down rivers, apparently, were naturally handy; the right tool always just happened to be in the chest that had washed ashore and the places where they landed were amazingly rich in just the resources one needed to survive. My own thoughts, over a lunch of the remaining garden vegetables and the last of the pickles, turned not upon resourcefulness but thievery. I would have to sneak back to the farmyard in the night and help myself to a few supplies. If Crusoe could ransack ships, why couldn't I have a go at the toolshed? I'd return the stuff, of course, when I had finished with it.

After lunch I took a nap. I was a free boy now, and such luxuries were available to me. Then I needed to think about supper. My life as a hunter and gatherer had begun. My first thought was to catch a fish. I didn't much like fish, but it was the only game I was prepared to catch. I whittled a digging stick and poked around in the soft furrows of the cornfield until I exposed a couple of earthworms, baited my hook, and tossed it out into a muskrat channel. Later, I could see, I was going to have to make a raft. It was a quiet, warm afternoon and nothing much was stirring, but it was pleasant to sit there imagining the huge bullhead that was about to strike.

There weren't any bullheads in the marsh, as I might have known if I had thought about it. I would have done better to have gone after a mess of crayfish, which abounded there, but I didn't yet know how delicious they are, and I had a profound fear of things that snapped. Once when I was much younger I found a flashlight bulb in a dresser drawer I had been told to stay out of and managed to swallow it. The next time I rummaged in that drawer, despite being sharply forbidden to do so by my mother, I got my fingers caught in the mousetrap that had been set there to teach me a lesson. Not only didn't I forget it, but it was years before I dared to get close again to anything that snapped. My grandmother had a case with a spring-loaded lid in which she kept her eyeglasses. I was terrified of it.

Eventually I despaired of catching a fish for my evening meal. What else might I find? Some corn. I went up into the field and picked a couple of ears. And frog legs! Why hadn't I thought of them before? They were, I had heard, a delicacy. If there is one thing a country boy knows, it is how to catch frogs. In short order, I had pounced upon two big leopard frogs and slaughtered them. After that, I was at a loss. Should one cook the whole carcass? Just the legs? Should they be skinned? How should they be cooked? The possibilities were mercifully limited. I severed the legs, found it difficult to get a grip on anything so small and slick, and so concluded that they must be cooked unskinned, boiled, obviously, since the only utensil I had was the tin can. I would have to think later how to pilfer a skillet. I made a fire, brought a bit of water to boil in the can, and dropped in the legs. While they cooked, I ate the raw corn. It was surprisingly good, I thought, even without salt and butter. Then I considered the legs, which had shriveled to almost nothing and turned an awful shade of gray. I poked at one of them with my knife, extracted a bit of flesh, swallowed it without tasting, and gagged anyway. Perhaps I didn't want to eat dead frog legs after all.

This knowledge depressed me deeply. I could not have said what I was depressed about, but it was the realization that my escape into the wilderness of the slough was not practical, that the place was, rich as it seemed, too narrow in its resources to sustain me, and that I was unequipped to take advantage of even the resources it did offer. I had dreamed of a retreat into a world long past, but it was the present world, I saw, in which I would have to make my way.

I sat beneath the cottonwood tree as the dusk rose again from the earth and spread like smoke. I cut a length of green willow branch, as my grandfather had shown me, worked its bark loose and slipped it off, carved an airway and a series of sound chambers in the naked stem, made finger holes in the bark, and slipped it back onto the stem. With my crude flute I joined the blackbirds in a song to welcome the night.

Later, in the light of the moon, I gathered my things into the folds of the quilt, slung the bundle over my shoulder, and made my melancholy way back to the house. I felt sheepish when I arrived at the breakfast table the next morning and was relieved to be welcomed as if I had never been away. My parents, I realized, knew where I had been all along. I had been out hunting for the way home.

Ed Will's farm survives, of course — in the midlands, land does not appear or vanish in a human lifetime. But it is now a kind of desert. The fencerows are gone. The house is gone. The marsh is gone. It was underlain with plastic drain tiles that now siphon its waters into a nearby drainage ditch, which carries them to the Minnesota River, which is connected to the Mississippi River, taking the fertile waters I once knew directly to the sea. The tile intakes in the bottom of the old marsh are marked by steel fence posts on which white plastic petroleum and chemical bottles hang, making them visible to the operators of the big machines that turn its soil. On the rises above the marsh the soils are now thin enough that the moldboards of the plows bring yellow patches of clay to the surface. The waterfowl are gone, the raptors are gone, the burrowing animals are gone, the predators and herbivores are gone. The insects that remain are learning to become specialists in the two or three domestic crops that now grow there. Some of them, like the grasshoppers, come and go in plagues. All across the township, the domestic animals are gone and the few barns that still stand are slowly imploding from their own weight. Last season, the whole 160 acres of what used to be our farm was planted with a single crop—corn.

There is hardly a desert so barren. I went walking once on a ranch in the Sonoran Desert, where it takes four or five farms the size of the one we had to raise a single cow. It was, in comparison, an oasis, supporting even a few mosquitoes; how, I cannot imagine. It ought to go without saying, but doesn't, that the people are gone from our farms, too. Do we think that we can plow a piece of land to its last square inch without also uprooting ourselves? Do we think that we are machines too?

If there is no one left to witness the way from Section 28, Rosewood Township, into the wide universe —and there scarcely is—does the connection still exist?

# The Transfiguration of Bread

ONE EVENING when one thing after another had gone wrong, Mother opened the cupboard door and a dinner plate crashed to the floor and shattered. Enraged by the perfidy of the plate, she pulled the others out of the cupboard one at a time and smashed them to the floor, too. She had begun demolishing the cups and saucers before she spent her anger. We children, already seated at the table for supper, watched in terror; sometimes Mother took her anger out on us.

She wept, dried her tears, swept up the shards, and served supper in soup bowls. My sisters and I ate in silence, excused ourselves, and went to bed early. For months after that, the family ate everything out of those soup bowls, each meal a reminder, like a festering wound, of that night. There was no money to buy replacement plates. After the harvest, when the money was finally found, we were all able to laugh about such a luxury as new plates, but I never forgot that night, nor, I think, did my mother.

This is one memory I carry of what it means to be poor, but it is not the only one, nor the dominant one. We were, by monetary standards, poor, but we were not, by any reasonable standard of physical need, impoverished.

We worked hard, although not so hard, in fact, as our more modern neighbors. We toiled when the sun was up, rested when it was not, and took Sundays off, while all around us at planting and harvest times the machines rumbled late into the night and Sundays were on their way to becoming ordinary days in the relentless turning of the weeks. As elsewhere in society, our labor-saving machines delivered not so much freedom from drudgery as enslavement to creditors.

Because we raised our own food, we always had an adequate supply; because our fuel was harvested from our own land, we were always warm and dry; because we had acquired little, we had little to lose. We experienced such joys and such sorrows as are the lot of all humanity. Our lives were not idyllic—far from it—but neither were they mean or oppressive. Still, it is possible to believe, despite countervailing evidence, that money alone, and only money, can supply life's sufficiencies, or, in the reverse, that to be in want of money is in itself degrading.

One early reader of this book, recalling the dreary novels of Hamlin Garland, reminded me of the "drudgery, tedium, and soul-destroying poverty" of preindustrial rural life and suggested that I was perpetuating "the myth of a golden age in agriculture," "the myth of the cheerful yeomanry," "a pastoral paradise." I don't, in fact, believe in such myths, nor, for that matter, do I know of anybody who does. These are not myths in any functional sense, but shibboleths. I keenly recall the tedium and drudgery of the life I knew as a child. But my own children, who have grown up in affluence, are also loudly cognizant of the tedium and drudgery in *their* lives. And I remember, as do they, many joys and satisfactions. I do not believe that the state of one's soul is in direct relation to the condition of one's bank balance. Wealth is as fully capable of corrupting the soul as poverty.

The primary human-development issues, one would think, have to do with physical and emotional security: do people have shelter from the weather, enough food, clothing adequate to the climate, a reasonable prospect of living to maturity, freedom from random violence? At the next level of development the questions ought to be about achieving one's creative potential: do the physical and emotional circumstances of one's life allow leisure from one's labors — time to love, to dance, to sing, to make poems, to meditate, to play with one's children, to converse with one's friends and neighbors? Only to the extent that money enhances these possibilities, and to the extent that it is equitably distributed in a society, so that the advantages of a few do not oppress the potential of the many, is the accumulation of wealth an appropriate or useful ambition.

The per capita gross national product of a nation, often interpreted as a reliable indicator of human health and happiness, is, by such standards, an extremely crude tool. As a measure of the comfort of individual lives, it is about as apt, say, as deciding how to dress in the morning according to the mean annual temperature of the region in which one lives. If one lives in the tropics this would work well. But if one lives in Minnesota, where the temperature might be thirty degrees below zero one morning and one hundred degrees above zero another morning, one would be in danger of dying of exposure or of prostration most of the time. The problem with aggregate statistics is that they obscure both the extremes and patterns of distribution.

Leaving the farm and poverty behind, I migrated as a young man to Washington, D.C., where I expected to make my fame and fortune. Within three hours of arriving in town, I was mugged. My wife and I lived in an English basement apartment whose half-windows, barred like prison windows, admitted a dim light and whose triple-locked doors secured us against intruders. Despite such measures, in six months we had been robbed twice. A visitor upstairs, the janitor at the church behind us, and my wife were beaten by thieves. The house on the corner opposite us was firebombed. We had no car, and cabs would not come to our address at night. If we wanted to go out in the evening, we had to walk several dark and terrifying blocks to a busy street to hail one. We seldom felt up to the effort. My wife, who had a job as a science writer, soon learned that she was expected to type her male colleagues' manuscripts as well as her own. My own job on Capitol Hill was thrilling and my co-workers splendid, but I was ill suited to the work and miserable about my inadequacies. I had long taken solace in walks, and the lovely countryside of nearby Maryland and Virginia beckoned, but I had no way to

get there. Ironically, my wife and I were both hand-
somely compensated for our labors. We had, in fact,
more money than we could use.

One night a lovesick tomcat cried in the window
well next to our front door. I had reached such a state of
paranoia that I thought it was a human baby somebody
had put there to trick us into opening the door. That
night I overcame the delusion, which I had nursed in
poverty, that if I had enough money, I might be happier.

The only acute pain that I can recall suffering because of my family's poverty was the intense humiliation
I felt when I discovered, as an adolescent, that most
people lived another way and that there was something
shameful, so far as others were concerned, about the way
we lived. I was embarrassed to invite my friends to our
house, which I had thought cozy and warm until I was
made to see it as dirty and bare.

Bread was the issue over which we children voiced
our new-found shame. Ours was home baked, using
wheat raised and ground on the farm, leavened with
home-cultured yeast, and sweetened with honey made
by the bees we kept at the bottom of our garden. It was
fabulous bread; almost every year it won my mother a
purple ribbon at the Chippewa County fair. The slicing
of the first loaf in a new batch, still steaming, its sweet,
nutty aroma filling the kitchen, was one of the sacred
rituals of our household.

But my sisters and I, driven by the collapse of rural
society out of our local school and into the consolidated
town school, had tasted the allure of a new world. We
had acquired the preference of the age for anything
manufactured over anything homemade. We suddenly
coveted boughten bread, contrived from flour so de-
nuded of its essence that its only nutrients came from

artificial additives. We were no longer content to eat hick bread. "Wonder Bread builds strong bodies seven ways," we said, proud of our familiarity with modern advertising slogans. We yammered and complained, I am ashamed to confess, until Mother finally gave up baking bread, and we began to eat, like modern folk, a factory substitute.

The real poverty that we then experienced, but did not recognize, characterizes the impoverishment that befell every aspect of rural culture with the industrialization of farming. Not only our palates suffered, not only our bodies, deprived of wholesome bread, but our very souls. Our souls depended in ways we had not anticipated upon the sanctity of the labors that brought bread to our table. We lost the ceremony and artfulness, in which every member of the family had some vital role, that once attended the eating of the grain: the planting and tilling, the harvesting and winnowing, the grinding and mixing, the miracle of its rising, the mystery of the transforming fire, the sacrament of the first loaf. Making bread was a critical element in the purpose of our lives, and one of the ways by which we were literally joined to the land. It was at the center of our culture, a civilizing force.

The Latin word from which our own word *culture* derives has several meanings: to inhabit, to till, to worship; these are, in fact, although we have forgotten it, intimately related actions. To inhabit a place means, if one is attentive to the idea from which the word comes, not simply to occupy it, or merely to own it, but to dwell within it, to have joined oneself in some organic way to it; it is the place where one's heart lives. The word *till* comes from an Old English word meaning to strive after, to get. The word *worship* is a contraction: it was originally *worth*ship, the homage one paid to whatever one valued.

So the idea of culture encompasses not only the arts and inventions of a people, but also the place within which they dwell, all that they strive after, and everything that they find worthy.

When we gave up the baking of bread in our household, we abandoned more than a habit of living; in a subtle but real way, we turned our backs upon our culture; and to that extent our lives became less worshipful. The wholesome mystery of bread, the sacrament of it, I know now, was never in the ingredients but in the labor, and in the laborers who transfigured them into bread.

# Remember
the Flowers

MY FATHER married and went into business for himself in the spring of 1946, raising laying hens, vegetables, and berries on a seven-acre truck farm. For the rest of his life he devoted as much time and care to his gardens and orchards and bee hives as to his crops. The eggs he sold to the local candling plant, the berries and vegetables to the local groceries. It was hard labor, mostly done with his hands and a two-wheeled garden tractor, and it afforded a meager living. By 1947 he had not only a wife but infant twins.

Sometimes it took all the eggs in the hen house to buy milk for the babies. In 1950, he rented 160 acres of land on shares. The move required investing in an ancient collection of farm machinery, but it also brought a barn and an above-ground house with three rooms and electricity; previously, the family lived in an unfinished basement. A decade later, my mother inherited eighty acres, giving our family the leverage to finance the purchase of an additional 120 acres of land, about forty acres of it in pasture and meadow. So my father became in the last ten years of his life a landholding farmer, although still on a small scale.

The 1950s and 1960s were a time of great expansion in American agriculture, significantly fueled by the introduction in 1947 of 2,4-D, an herbicide that was to become a cheap alternative to the labor of cultivation. It had predictable consequences, although they were not predicted. One was overproduction. By the late 1950s, the Soil Bank had become part of the language of agriculture, the measuring wheels of the inspectors from the Agricultural Stabilization and Conservation Service one of its tools, and the ranks of steel bins brimming with unmarketable grain one of its monuments. We had created a fantastic new food machine, like Strega Nona's pasta pot, but nobody knew how to turn it off.

My father disregarded the new agriculture. He did not want land he could not care for. He refused to use the new chemicals. He was certain they were dangerous in ways that we would eventually understand. In any case, they required cash, and all a hoe cost was labor, of which he already had an adequate supply. At a time when a farmer's manhood was expressed in the size of his machines, he bought the smallest Fordson tractor available, a machine so insignificant that even I, a child, was embarrasssed to drive it.

At a time when monoculture was the fashion, he diversified. He expanded the sheep herd, started a business in goat's milk for families with infants allergic to cow's milk, planted potatoes and cucumbers, began a big orchard, and trapped muskrats and mink in the winter. When the neighbors were razing the groves of empty farmsteads to make more land, he planted pines. When they tiled their meadows and plowed them, he dug a new pond in his for wild ducks.

He was not indifferent to success. He studied the bulletins from the Agricultural Extension Service as assiduously as anybody. All winter, he pored over the reports of crop variety trials, making notes of new hybrids to try. He kept his own careful performance records in the pocket notebooks handed out by the seed companies. He had a soil-testing kit and used it religiously. He meant to be the best farmer possible. He just didn't see the connection between farming well and getting rich.

I had grown to adolescence and seen something of the world. He made me furious. He was so old-fashioned, so shamelessly willing to be different. One day I shouted at him, "You are like the soldier in the army who insists that everyone else is out of step!" I thought myself awfully clever.

He stared back at me, white with contempt. "Have you ever considered," he said, "the possibility that the soldier may be right?"

My father, I suppose, could be dismissed as impractical. I dimly remember the search for a suitable piece of land when it became possible for him to buy one. He wanted two others much more than he wanted the farm he actually bought. One came with a single building on a treeless hillside, a European-style farmhouse: house, barn, and henhouse were all attached under a single roof, so that one could open a door and walk directly from the upstairs bedrooms into the hayloft and from there down through a trap-door into the animal quarters. We children were enthralled. There was an argument in the car on the way home. "Think how efficient it would be," Father said.

"Absolutely not," Mother said. "I will not live in a pigsty! You buy it and you can go live there without me."

It was clear that she meant it.

The other was a farm lying in river-bottom land. The house on it was about to collapse. It was in worse condition than the house we were then living in. On the way home from our inspection visit, Father sounded childishly excited, the only time I ever saw him in such a state. Mother said nothing, but halfway home she began to cry.

The first farm attracted my father because it included an enormous slough, the second because it was next to the river and consisted mainly of woodlands and rocky pastures. There were farmers who thought that the most beautiful thing in the world was a flat field turned so thoroughly in the fall that nothing not perfectly black showed in it; who labored and conspired to employ every square inch of earth at their disposal; who tore out fences, cut down stray trees, drained marshes, plowed up farmyards and road ditches, abandoned waterways in a desperate effort to wring the last dime out of a property; who saw any untilled acre as an offense against industriousness. But my father cherished the acres he couldn't farm as much as the ones he planted. He would no more have thought of buying a farm without any waste space than of moving to New York City and becoming a belly dancer.

We pulled into the yard at home after our trip to the farm along the river. Father turned to Mother, who was staring out the window, refusing to look at him, and said,

"I suppose you're right, honey. I suppose it really isn't practical." But I could tell that he said it out of resignation, not out of conviction.

Even now, when the fruits of farming as an industrial enterprise lay like so many rotting apples on the land, there are people who say that there is nothing wrong with agriculture that a better price for corn couldn't fix. They are right. If our success is to be measured solely in profit margins, let us guarantee the price of corn at $10 a bushel or $100 a bushel—it hardly matters what the figure is—and get on with our lives. Land prices will soar, and so will land abuse and the prices that suppliers charge. Rural population will continue to dwindle. The communities that survive will continue to struggle to maintain decently vigorous local institutions. Every issue of short-term justice and long-term sanity will remain. But those few who survive in farming will become rich and powerful beyond even their wildest dreams.

We in rural America have a long list of enemies. The government did it to us. The bankers did it to us. The grain cartels did it to us. The professors of agriculture did it to us. They did, but we have had no agricultural policy that somebody in agriculture didn't press for, and no lousy piece of advice ever came to fruition except when somebody agreed to take it. The question every farmer has to answer, Wendell Berry once said, is this: "Would you rather have your neighbor's land or your neighbor?" We have made the choice over and over again, and if we now have very few neighbors, we must allocate some portion of the blame to ourselves. There was always another choice.

The heart of the matter is the question of economy. There are, essentially, only two ways to balance a checkbook. One is to make more, and the other is to make do with less. Of course there are limits to the second strategy. Even Thoreau kept three chairs in his shack at Walden Pond. "None is so poor that he need sit on a pumpkin," he said, although I once lived in a house where we sat on empty sauerkraut kegs and am not aware that it did me or anyone else any harm.

My father lived in an industrial economy that he did not entirely spurn. He acquired property, purchased goods and services, participated in government farm programs, and received public support for his participation, without, so far as I am aware, any regret. He believed in government and in its duty, not to mention its privilege, to manage our common affairs for the greatest general good.

We had a serious falling-out over this issue during the Vietnam War. I refused to fight, believing the war immoral; my father believed just as passionately that I was wrong, that I could seek in every legal way to change the government's policy, but so long as it was the policy, he said, I had a moral and a Christian duty to follow it. During this time, I gave a speech arguing otherwise. My father listened to it on the radio, and when I went to the farm afterwards to see him, he met me at the front door and told me coldly that I was not welcome, that traitors were never welcome at his house. He was no isolationist, no believer in a world where it is every man for himself.

He did, nevertheless, practice a personal economy that was at considerable odds with the public economy. He tried to do as much for himself as possible. In part, this meant being handy. He was not much of a consumer, but he spent a good deal of time at the local implement dealerships, studying the latest innovations and borrowing whatever ideas he found useful. He made an occasional visit to the blacksmith's shop for a bit of

ironwork he wasn't equipped to handle, but otherwise
he was self-sufficient. He was his own mechanic, his own
carpenter, his own electrician, his own soil scientist, his
own feed formulator, his own miller, his own veterinar-
ian. He probably died so young because he insisted, until
it was too late, on being his own doctor. When he wanted
something, he made it. If he couldn't make it, he did
without, or invented an alternative.

We raised our own food. Doing so saved money, my
father enjoyed the work, and he had available—a fact I
came as a child to rue—a ready supply of labor. It
seemed to him so logical, so obvious a thing to do that
the rarity of home food production mystified him. That's
what farmers do, he said, they raise food. If I am a
farmer, he asked, and cannot feed even myself, what sort
of farmer am I? Should a tailor hire somebody to make
his own clothes? Should a cobbler send his own shoes
out to be fixed? So he raised livestock for meat and milk,
kept bees for honey, chickens for eggs, maintained an orchard for fruit, tended vegetable and berry gardens,
raised wheat and ground it himself into flour. He didn't
have the imagination to do less.

In his economy the guiding principle was the avoid-
ance of waste. He understood the word to mean the
unnecessary expenditure of life or its resources. Idling
acres to curb excess production, therefore, made sense to
him, but dumping milk didn't. Idle land was not wasted,
but merely lying fallow. Rest benefitted the land and was,
in any case, of some use to God's creation. But to spend
resources to produce food which you then threw out
merely because you couldn't make a profit on it, that to
him was waste, a kind of blasphemy. In the same way, it
seemed to him not merely practical but moral to heat our
house with wood. Wood was, after all, available to us for

the labor of harvesting it. Why should we burn coal, exhaustible and needing to be dug by somebody else, when we were capable of supplying our own replenishable heat at no expense to anyone else? Shouldn't the coal be reserved for those who had no better alternative? My father's goal in economic matters, as in the rest of life, was to trouble others as little as possible.

I think he also meant to be as little trouble to himself as possible. He simplified his economic life so that the rest of his life might also be freed. In this he was Thoreauvian, although he never read Thoreau; his habits, I think, gave our neighbors the same sort of trouble that Thoreau's gave his.

My father worked diligently at farming, but he refused to work at it slavishly. He rose at sunrise, but never earlier, and, at least in the summertime, frequently went to bed shortly after sundown. He believed in long, leisurely meals, napped after lunch, and kept the Sabbath faithfully. Sometimes our neighbors, particularly during the planting and harvesting seasons, rose long before daylight and worked late into the night, the headlights of their machines piercing the midnight blackness. But when it got dark, the work on our farm stopped, no matter what the urgency of time or weather. I myself, as a teenager, rose at 4:30 in the morning in the summertime to work one job, took a break for lunch, and then frequently worked a second job until 10 or 10:30 in the evening. My father did not intervene, but he made it perfectly clear that he regarded the practice as madness, as I myself now do.

He believed that a life of constant toil was badly led, a life God never intended for anyone. His farming was important to him, a noble and sacred calling. But he also attended the flowering of wild plants, the singing of

birds, the swarming of bees, the trails of foxes. He culti-
vated his gardens. He walked in the woods. He prayed
and meditated. In the winter, he helped his children to
make igloos and snow tunnels. In the summer, he held
them in his arms under the stars and sang to them in his
sweet, shy tenor voice.

For several years, we raised a couple of acres of cucumbers, an important cash crop. The project involved
the entire family. It might have been an unbearable
drudgery. After the ground was plowed in the spring,
everything was done by hand. The seeds were hand
planted in handmade hills, the patch was weeded with
hoes, and during the harvest season we all spent three
mornings a week, beginning before the dew had dried,
picking the cucumbers one by one, filling a peck basket,
dumping it into the truck parked at the end of the field,
filling another peck, and another, and another, until we
were green and sticky to our elbows with the rank juice
of cucumber vines and the sun was high and suffocat-
ingly hot. It was backbreaking work, the more so because
it had to be done meticulously. The cucumbers were
graded by size; the bigger they got, the less we were paid
for them.

When we had gleaned the field, we hauled the cucumbers to the buying station in Willmar, forty miles
away. We all piled into the truck, grateful for the chance
simply to sit, and after we had sold the day's harvest, we
retired to a lake near Willmar, swam away the late afternoon, picnicked in the shade of an oak tree, and drove
home at dusk, singing songs or falling happily asleep on
our parents' shoulders. In my father's economy, those
half days lounging at the lake were as vital as the mornings spent in the cucumber patch. Without the one, he
would not have suffered the other.

Sometimes this attitude resulted in a casualness toward life that could seem callous. One fall morning after we children had gone to school, the creosote in the chimney of our house caught fire and started a blaze in the attic. Father was miles away, on his parents' farm, plowing. Mother was home alone. She ran to the neighbors', borrowed the telephone, called the fire department, and then called Grandmother and asked her to fetch Father. The fire truck came, Grandmother came, the neighbors came, but not my father.

He worked, as usual, until noon and then returned for lunch, uncertain, of course, whether there was any lunch to be had. My sister and I also walked home from school for lunch. We were horrified when we rounded the grove, saw the commotion of neighbors and firemen in the yard, and realized what had happened. Father arrived after us. When Mother noticed him, she turned on him, the only time, I think, that she defied him in public. "Where have you been?" she shouted.

"I have been plowing the eighty," he said calmly.

"While our house was burning!"

"I know that," he said, "but there was nothing I could do to stop it, was there? And I had work to do."

She was stunned into silence.

He never understood why she was so angry, or why his behavior was inexcusable. As far as he was concerned, you worried about what you could change, and you accepted everything else. If a house burned, it was, after all, only a house.

Thoreau went to Walden Pond, he said, to conduct an experiment. "I went to the woods because I wanted to live deliberately, to front out only the essential facts of life, and to see if I could not learn what it had to teach, and not, when I came to die, discover that I had not lived." He was explicit about the nature of his experiment. It was not, he said, a model for the ideal life, not an experiment he meant anybody else to copy: "I would not have anyone adopt *my* mode of living on any account; for, beside that before he has fairly learned it I may have found out another for myself, I desire that there may be as many different persons in the world as possible; but I would have each one be very careful to find and pursue *his own* way, and not his father's or his mother's or his neighbor's instead." What his experiment taught him had nothing to do with living "cheaply or meanly." The lesson was in values, not in prices:

*I learned this, at least, by my experiment: that if one advances confidently in the direction of his dreams, and endeavors to live the life which he has imagined, he will meet with a success unexpected in common hours. He will put some things behind, will pass an invisible boundary; new, universal, and more liberal laws will begin to establish themselves around and within him; or the old laws be expanded, and interpreted in his favor in a more liberal sense, and he will live with the license of a higher order of beings. In proportion as he simplifies his life, the laws of the universe will appear less complex, and solitude will not be solitude, nor poverty poverty, nor weakness weakness. . . . Superfluous wealth can buy superfluities only. Money is not required to buy one necessary of the soul.*

Thoreau's experiment has raised a nervous defensiveness in a long line of critics. We have a public conception of moral responsibility. Despite the long thread of individualism running through our culture, we tend to believe that what is good is good in the collective sense. We may admire Thoreau and his descendents for the high-mindedness of their sentiments, but we are at the same time suspicious of a philosophy that seems so personal, so intensely directed at the individual life. To seek by public means to change the evil in our lives is something we can honor and respect. But simply to refuse, as one human being acting alone, to participate in evil, that seems to us somehow dangerous, selfish, too piddling to make a practical difference. How could Thoreau, we want to know, busy himself, in good conscience, as the "self-appointed inspector of snow-storms and rainstorms" when the far greater turbulence of slavery was raging all around? It is true that he championed John Brown, spoke passionately in Concord and elsewhere in favor of abolition, and perhaps assisted a traveler or two on the underground railway to freedom in Canada, but it is also true that Thoreau was no civil reformer. His heart wasn't in it. He would sooner have gone walking in the woods than have organized a political action. How dare such a man pretend to moral superiority?

There are two classes of moralists: those who seek to improve the quality of other people's lives and those who are content to improve their own lives. There are professors of morality, and there are practitioners of it; and the categories tend to be exclusive. Nothing is so terrifying as a demonstration of principle. Emerson preached Nature; Thoreau embraced nature. It is Thoreau, of course, who ultimately strikes us as dangerous. It is one thing to decry the rat race. That is the good and honorable work of moralists. It is quite another to drop out, to refuse to run any farther. That is the work of the individualist, and it is offensive because it makes the rebuke personal; the individualist calls not someone else's behavior into question, but mine. The moralist believes in the necessity of enemies, the individualist in their irrelevance.

My father went to the same church as the rest of us, confessed the same creed, partook of the same absolution. He heard the same preaching: "Take no thought for the morrow," and "Lay not up treasures on earth, where moth and rust doth corrupt," and "It is harder for a rich man to enter into heaven than for a camel to pass through the eye of a needle." He made people nervous because he not only professed such beliefs, he practiced them. Such a man will keep on plowing even when he hears that his house is burning. People said of him what is always said of such people: How selfish, how impractical, what a shame for his family! Think what he might have done if he had ever tried to make anything of himself!

One spring night my father went to bed, fell asleep, and never awoke. He died as quietly, as uncomplainingly, as he lived. It was an awkward moment for a farmer to die, too late in the season to secure someone else to run the land. He knew he was dying. In the papers he left behind were a set of instructions for Mother: diagrams of the farm, notes on what to plant where and when, instructions on the management and harvest of the crops, on the care of the machinery, on the arcane details of the year's farm program, everything Mother needed to know in order to operate the farm herself that summer, as she did, triumphantly.

Among the instructions as well was a plan for the flower beds in the yard, complete with planting charts, species names, and notes about when each variety would bloom and what color it would be. Even when facing death the flowers mattered to him. They were a reminder, which I have sometimes betrayed but never forgotten, of all that is genuinely important in life.

**2**

# Corn
# Is Not
# Eternal

ONLY A LITTLE MORE THAN
a century ago, there lived in
Rosewood Township a people who
had staked their lives and fortunes
upon the buffalo. The buffalo
once flourished in seemingly in-
exhaustible numbers. There
were, perhaps, sixty million of them. When Coronado,
the first European to see the prairies, traveled to Kansas
in 1541, a journey of several months, he reported that
he was never once beyond sight of them.

If you were born into plains culture in those days,
you were wrapped in swaddling clothes made from the

soft skin of a buffalo calf and carried about until you could walk in a cradle lined with the pulverized dung of the buffalo, which served as a diaper. You grew into an adult life dependent in every particular upon the buffalo. It supplied you with food, with raiment, with shelter, with tools, with household furnishings, with paints and dyes, with cosmetics, with fuel. And when you died, you were buried, or raised upon a platform, in a coffin made of buffalo hide. The buffalo was literally the beginning and the ending of your existence. You would have believed that the buffalo was eternal.

And then came the Europeans, whose railroad lines and fences and plows and relentless hunting reduced the buffalo nearly to extinction. This decimation threatened the survival of plains culture, as Americans knew. The United States Congress passed a bill in the 1860s to protect the few hundred buffalo that still survived, out of the tens of millions. President Grant vetoed it on the advice of his secretary of war, who said that to get rid of the buffalo was to get rid of the Indian problem.

There arose, then, among the desperate Native Americans, a shaman who said that the buffalo had not died, that they had merely gone down into the safety of the underworld. If the people, the shaman preached, would say the right prayers and perform the right dances, the buffalo would return and their way of life would be saved. So all across the prairies, the people danced and prayed. But Americans, despite their constitution, outlawed this new aspect of native religions, the Ghost Dance.

In South Dakota, in December of 1890, a group of Lakota Sioux danced in defiance of the ban. When ordered to quit, they left their reservation and headed for the Badlands, where they could dance and pray in peace.

Along the way, they were set upon by American cavalry
and slaughtered, men, women, and children alike. The
few survivors were carried to a nearby mission and laid
out on the sanctuary floor to be treated for their wounds.
Above the altar, hung for the Christmas season, was a
banner reading, "Peace on Earth, Good Will Toward
Men." The place was Wounded Knee.

This was the last battle of a long war. The buffalo
were not, after all, eternal.

Today we have made, in places like Rosewood
Township, a culture as dependent upon corn as Sioux
culture was upon buffalo. A person born in our time will
as an infant be clothed in a diaper made in part of corn
and fed a formula based upon corn syrup. That person
will grow into adult life sustained in thousands of ways by
products made from, packaged in, or manufactured with
derivatives of corn, from every kind of food except fresh
fish to plastics, textiles, building materials, machine
parts, soaps and cosmetics, even highways. And when
that person dies, some laws require that the body should
be embalmed—in a fluid made in part from corn.

We have not begun to imagine a life without corn.
We have assumed, by the default of failing to think about
it, that corn is eternal. But it is not any more eternal than
the buffalo. In fact, because the corn we cultivate shares
a common cytoplasm, it would take exactly one persistent pathogen to devastate our culture as we know it.

# Snails
# Have
# Faces

W ARM WEATHER brings the pleasure
of nature walks with children. I
like the exuberance of children on
such walks, the way they take small
things seriously, their unjaded acceptance of the everyday world as
a place still waiting to be discovered.

The world still is undiscovered, as a matter of fact,
until you have found its secrets for yourself, but only children (and some artists) seem to understand this with any
conviction. They don't delegate the work of discovery.
They boldly assume it for themselves. When I go walking

with children, thinking to show them a bit of the natural world, I usually end up learning something about my own understanding of it.

"Here," I say, "is catnip. Your pet cat or rabbit loves to munch on it, and so do I."

The children do not nod politely and pass on to the next object. They try catnip on their own tongues. "Eeuuw," one of them says. "It's bitter."

"It is, a little," I say. "Don't you like it?"

"Yuck, no!"

We approach a marsh. A red fox bolts. I am thrilled. Not often can you produce a red fox in the field for fifty chattering third-graders. They seem unimpressed. But after that the children see phantom foxes on every distant hillside. They have already learned the visual pattern of a fox running in a field and are determined to find it for themselves. It does not matter whether there are actually any foxes out there. One day, soon enough, there will be.

In the clear, shallow water at the edge of the pond the children are captivated, as I always have been, by the pond snails floating on the surface. They fish them up in their hands.

"Snails have faces, you know," I say.

We turn a snail on end, find its big flat foot and, forward of it, the eyestalks and tiny mouth edged with Lilliputian teeth. Children believe that a snail has eyes only when they have peered into them with their own, demanding, subconsciously, I suppose, the verification of experience. My statement — a snail has a face, you know — is received not as a fact but as an interesting proposition worth testing. I am granted, among a group of children, the authority to raise questions but not necessarily the right to proclaim truth.

They ask their own questions. What does a snail eat? Does it sleep? Where does it go at night? How old does it get? How does it go to the bathroom? I am brought up against the limits of my own knowledge with discomforting abruptness.

Children want to touch everything, to smell the flowers, taste the leaves, dangle their feet in the water, pick apart the scat, carry home the bones. Sometimes I am impatient about this desire for direct contact. "Have respect!" I want to say. But in the end I hold my tongue, knowing they pay their respects by making sensual contact with the world. "The opposite of love," a friend reminds me, "is not hatred, but indifference."

I heard the other day what that indifference sounds like to a child. I was walking along the lake where I live when a little boy came running to his mother with the shell of a clam that he had picked up on the shore. "Look! Look, Mommy! See what I've found!" the child said, brandishing the clamshell.

"Put that down. This instant. Do you hear me? Put that dirty old thing back where you found it!" She yelled at him.

The baffled boy did as he was told. It is a hard thing to learn to be indifferent to the world, but, unfortunately, we have many instructors. I think of the baby I saw being slapped the other night for exploring the sound of a few pebbles falling from her hand onto the bumper of her daddy's car. I think of the teacher who assured me that everybody knows following procedure is more important than acquiring any piece of information about the world.

After we have walked for an hour or so, the same thing always happens. A child comes forward and takes my hand. Then someone clasps my other hand and we walk, the three of us, palm against palm. No child ever asks permission. The warm, soft hands, offered so confidently, feel trusting and loving.

Sometimes on a passage through a woods or along a road one of the children will clutch my hand a little tighter and tell me something urgent.

"I have no mother."

"What happened?"

"She died. When I was five."

I don't know how to respond. I think perhaps I'm not meant to do more than to witness the bald fact of a sorrow plainly expressed.

But I do wonder what provokes such intimacy in these circumstances. I think the posture involved in walking in wild places induces it. I always begin a hike with a little talk about the art of really observing a natural landscape. I tell the children it's their place and they can approach it in any way that they like. But if you really want to see something, I say, you must first be silent. Then I describe the naturalist's habit of using peripheral vision to watch for the tiny movements that signal the presence of another creature. And early in a walk we stop to smell a flower, examine a track, taste a leaf or berry, to consider some object that can be passed from hand to hand.

The point, of course, is to awaken the senses, to stimulate alertness and concentration. I want, through the shock of visceral contact, to draw the children out of themselves and into the world. Once, faced with a classroom full of students too self-conscious to write, I brought a bag of yellow onions, cut them open, and passed them around until the whole room reeked of onions and the tears were flowing freely. The students suddenly found a way to reach into the world. They wrote about onions, but then about all the other things that make them cry: losses, slights, injustices, moments of love and beauty. I apply the same idea to myself when my own work is stymied by private cares. I put aside whatever I have been doing (or avoiding) and go for a walk too long for comfort. When I return I find that my sight has been restored.

There is, as I say, a posture to this. It is wide-eyed, erect, open eared. Such posture straightens you up, slows you down, and focuses every particle of your sensory system on all the particulars of the world at your feet. It is a way of exposing yourself to the wonder in the world. Among those wonders is the possibility of taking a teacher firmly by the hand and sharing with him something he ought to know but doesn't.

I walk with the children, attached to one of them by my right hand, to another by my left, and to still others who have by now latched onto us and made a human chain. Every few yards we stop to examine some fresh discovery made along a perfectly ordinary path. The children exclaim and fire questions but don't necessarily accept the answers, if, that is, I have answers to give.

The day is growing long and the sun has begun to stare into our eyes. The children's legs are growing tired. I hope that I never weary of them. I hope that they never become sated with the world. What wonderful citizens they might make!

But, more likely, one by one they will fall out of love with the world. One day most of them will think they have seen it all. They will forget the posture of discovery. Eventually, they will no longer remember how to ask questions. They will only know how to state opinions.

Then they will run up against a tough, practical problem—what to do, say, about hazardous wastes. They will gather in groups, but they will not take each other's hands or tell of urgent news from their hearts. They will utter opinions, keeping their distance, until the sun sets. In the darkness, they will call each other names. None of this will solve the problem.

What to do? They will summon an expert, any expert, and whatever they are told they will believe, because they are helplessly bloated with conventional wisdom and have forgotten how to question. Or, too tired of the world to think for themselves, they will delegate the responsibility for deciding to those who proclaim themselves authorities.

If they are lucky, however, one or two among them will still be as wise as a child, will not have learned everything, will not yet have discovered everything, and will rise and assume that boldest of adult responsibilities, the responsibility of asking a question or two without the slightest concern for appearing dumb or difficult. Perhaps, too, these one or two questioners will still have the determination of a child and not necessarily accept the answers they are given.

# What the Prairie Teaches Us

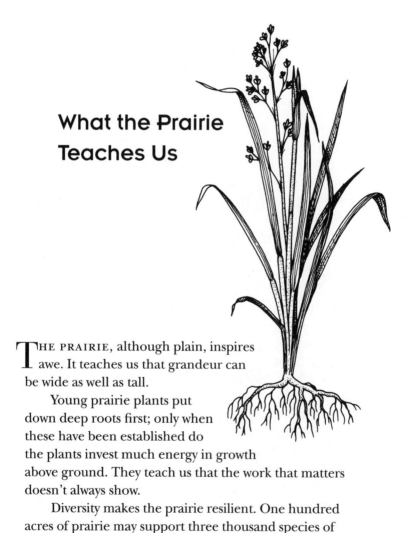

THE PRAIRIE, although plain, inspires awe. It teaches us that grandeur can be wide as well as tall.

Young prairie plants put down deep roots first; only when these have been established do the plants invest much energy in growth above ground. They teach us that the work that matters doesn't always show.

Diversity makes the prairie resilient. One hundred acres of prairie may support three thousand species of insects alone, each of them poised to exploit—often beneficially—certain plants, microclimates, soils, weather conditions, and seasons. This exuberance equips the prairie to make the most of every opportunity, to meet every natural contingency. The prairie teaches us to see our own living arrangements as stingy and to understand that this miserliness is why they so frequently fall short of our expectations.

The prairie is a community. It is not just a landscape or the name of an area on a map, but a dynamic alliance of living plants, animals, birds, insects, reptiles, and microorganisms, all depending upon each other. When too few of them remain, their community loses its vitality and they perish together. The prairie teaches us that our strength is in our neighbors. The way to destroy a prairie is to cut it up into tiny pieces, spaced so that they have no communication.

The prairie is patient. When drought sets in, as it inevitably does, prairie grasses bide their time. They do not flower without the nourishment to make good seed. Instead, they save their resources for another year when the rains have fallen, the seeds promise to be fat, and the earth is moist and ready to receive them. The prairie teaches us to save our energies for the opportune moment.

The prairie grows richer as it ages. Our own horticultural practices eventually deplete the soils. The topsoil washes or blows away; without additives, fertility dwindles. But the soils beneath the protective cover of prairie sod deepen over time; their tilth improves as burrowing animals and insects plow organic matter into them; fires recycle nutrients; deep roots bring up trace elements from the substrate; abundant legumes and microorganisms help to keep it fertile. The prairie was so effective at this work that, more than a century after it was broken, it remains the richest agricultural region in the world. The prairie teaches us how to be competitive without also being destructive.

The prairie is tolerant. There are thousands of species of living things on the prairie, but few of them are natives. The prairie has welcomed strangers of every kind and has borrowed ideas from all of its neighboring communities. In doing so, it has discovered how to flourish in a harsh place. The prairie teaches us to see the virtue of ideas not our own and the possibilities that newcomers bring.

The prairie turns adversity to advantage. Fires were frequent on the unplowed prairies. The prairie so completely adapted to this fact that it now requires fire for its health. Regular burning discourages weedy competitors, releases nutrients captured in leaves and stems, reduces thatch that would otherwise become a stifling mulch, stimulates cloning in grasses, and encourages the growth of legumes, which capture nitrogen from the air and make it available to the whole prairie community. The prairie teaches us to consider the uses that may be made of our setbacks.

The prairie is cosmopolitan. On the wings of winds and of birds, in the migrations of animals and insects, down the waters of streams and rivers come the messages, mainly contained in genetic codes, that sustain the prairie. Its storms swoop out of the Arctic or sweep up from the Gulf; many of its songbirds are familiar with the tropical rainforests; its monarch butterflies winter in the highlands of Mexico; its ducks vacation on seacoasts and in desert oases; its parasites hitchhike upon all of them. We think that we have discovered the global village, but the prairie knew of it millennia ago.

The prairie is bountifully utilitarian. But it is lovely

too, in a hundred thousand ways and in a million details, many of them so finely wrought that one must drop to one's knees to appreciate them. This is what, over all else, the prairie teaches us: there need be no contradiction between utility and beauty.

# What We Teach
# Rural Children

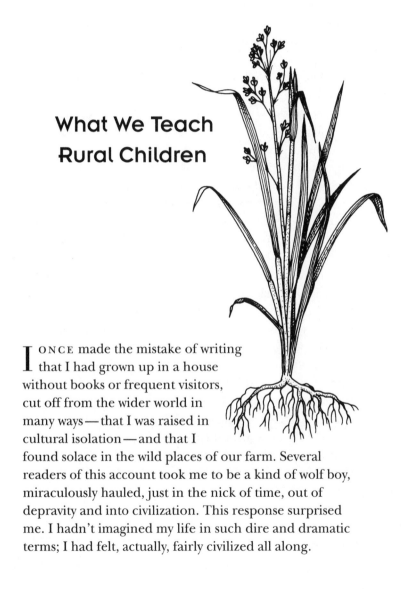

I ONCE made the mistake of writing
that I had grown up in a house
without books or frequent visitors,
cut off from the wider world in
many ways — that I was raised in
cultural isolation — and that I
found solace in the wild places of our farm. Several
readers of this account took me to be a kind of wolf boy,
miraculously hauled, just in the nick of time, out of
depravity and into civilization. This response surprised
me. I hadn't imagined my life in such dire and dramatic
terms; I had felt, actually, fairly civilized all along.

When I described the loneliness in my life—I called it the silence—I was not thinking of the scarcity of books in our house, much as I yearned for them. Nor did I have in mind the material simplicity of our existence. I was thinking, rather, about the rural community into which I was born but which had collapsed by the time I was a teenager, a decline heightened for me, no doubt, by the fact that we moved out of it during the dawning of my pubescence.

The move was toward prosperity. On the strength of a small inheritance, my parents had accumulated the capital to buy a place of their own after years of tenant farming. The new farm lay just a few miles west in the next township; we had not yet measured the psychological distance. The place not only belonged to us, but it had a house of seven ample rooms with tall windows and was in decent repair, unlike the three cramped and tumbledown rooms we had been used to. On winter mornings in that old house, we sometimes found drifts of powdery snow that the wind had driven through the cracks and that the kerosene stove had failed to melt. Our sturdy new house, seated on a lovely green bluff, was palatial by comparison. We had improved our station but not, it soon became clear, our lot in life. We had left our old neighborhood without moving into another. Our new neighbors were welcoming and kind; this was not an issue of civility. We had, rather, come up against a difficulty of timing.

One Sunday after the noon meal, we children were summoned to a rare family conference. "We have something to tell you," my mother said, looking strangely radiant, "but it is a secret, and you are not to tell anyone. Do you understand?"

"Yes," my sister and I said. "We understand. We won't tell."

"Remember, this is a secret," she said.

"Yes, yes," we said.

"Well," she said, "your father and I want you to know that we are going to have a baby. When winter comes, you will have a new little brother or sister. Isn't that wonderful? But this is a secret between us for now. Okay?"

"Okay!" we said, dancing with glee. We could hardly wait for Mother and Father to take their Sunday nap. (We had not yet discovered the connection between Sunday naps and new babies.) The instant they had settled down, we crept out the door, rushed to the next farm, and summoned the children.

"We have a secret," we said. "We have a secret." We stubbed our toes in the dirt, trying to look mysterious.

"Tell us! Tell us!"

What could we do, pressed as we were? "But don't tell anybody else," we said.

By nightfall it was common knowledge in the neighborhood: "The Gruchows are expecting. Next winter." That was in the 1950s.

We moved, as it happened, in the early 1960s, when the first fruits of farm industrialization had come to harvest. Consolidation was the word of the hour. Land holdings were being consolidated. The farmstead closest to our new house was vacant and growing up with weeds. The one across the section had already been razed and put to production. Schools were being consolidated, too. The rural neighborhood schools were the first to go, then the village schools. My great-grandfather had retired to a village just across the river valley that we could see from our front doorstep, but its school was already closed, as was almost everything else in the village, except the municipal bar, which did—perhaps not coincidentally—a booming business. We children had once only a hundred

yards to walk to our district schoolhouse. Now we trudged
through the winter darkness to the stop a quarter mile
away where we caught the bus for the long haul to the
nearest city school. Even rural churches could not escape
consolidation. We continued after our move to attend
church in our old neighborhood; there wasn't one in
Tunsberg Township. There were no children our age
within walking distance. They were by then disappearing
from our old neighborhood, too. Had our family conference taken place in the 1960s, the news of the baby would
likely have remained a secret. The gossip by then, in any
case, was of acquisitions, not of pregnancies.

After our move we were not lonely because we were
poor or because we lived in a house without books.
We were lonely because we no longer lived in a community. We had moved, for all practical purposes, into an
industrial park. Neither were we lonely because we lived
primitively. On the contrary, we lived at the cutting edge
of modernity.

In the decade of my coming of age, millions of farm
dwellers left the land and sought new lives in towns and
cities, not because that was what they desired but because they had no alternative. This removal constituted
one of the greatest mass migrations in history. Wendell
Berry has encapsulated it in the memorable phrase, "the
unsettling of America."

If you grew up on a farm in the last fifty years, as I
did, and were at all alert to what was happening there,
you could not have missed the steady attrition of all
kinds. You would have seen the empty farmhouses, the
barns rotting and falling in on themselves, the pink
trailer houses on concrete blocks replacing two-story
houses with veranda porches. You would have noticed
the diminishing songbirds, the disappearing butterflies,

the vanishing potholes, the uprooted fencerows, the
balding hilltops. You would have watched schoolhouses
become township halls, their playgrounds grown up with
weeds. You would have known that they were standing
empty not only because there were bigger schools elsewhere but also because there were fewer children. You
would have seen the arithmetic that went into the grocery lists your mother made on the backs of envelopes;
you would have seen the rows of items with their prices
and the sums at the bottom, and you would have ob-
served that items had been crossed out to make the
family's needs equal its resources, not the other way
around. You would have seen the empty churchyards.
Only the cemeteries remained, odd temples of death
jutting out of cornfields. You could still be buried in the
countryside, but you could no longer be baptized there.

If you listened to the radio or read the newspapers
or asked your vocational agriculture instructor at the
high school to explain what was happening, you would
have learned that the United States was experiencing a
modern miracle in the world's most efficient agriculture,
a way of farming so slick and fine that it didn't need
people anymore, or soils, or birds, or schoolhouses, or
children. All the miracle required was more petroleum
and bigger tractors and more land.

And you would have counted up, taken stock. If you
were at all bright, you could have read the bottom line.
You would have realized that you were among the items
no longer needed: you, or your parents, or your cousins,
or the neighbors down the road. The miracle being celebrated was your own obsolescence.

American agriculture settled after the Second World
War into a wearyingly rapid pattern of booms and busts.
After every bust you heard the same easy explanation

from the government analysts and the bank and the farm economists. America, they said, has been burdened with too many farmers. This latest bust has been painful, to be sure, they said, but also necessary and, in the long run, beneficial. We have been weeding out the poor and inefficient operators, they said. They did not say this— economists rarely speak so bluntly—but they meant it: We have been clearing the human trash out of farming. We have been making the countryside safe for machines.

Ours was a community, mainly, of second- and third-generation Germans and Norwegians. In the year of my birth it was still possible to attend a Norwegian-language church service, and the German prisoners of war who had been pressed into service as farm laborers had only recently departed. But our schools taught neither language and offered instruction in neither culture. We were to suppose that the Italian autoworkers of Detroit, the Polish beermakers of Milwaukee, and the Norwegian farmers of western Minnesota were culturally indistinguishable, that ethnicity was, if it was anything at all, a private matter of no consequence to the community.

We were also to suppose that there was no such thing in America as class. We all knew where the railroad tracks ran and who lived on which side of them, but in the classroom or in the pulpit nobody ever tried to articulate for us the difference between James J. Hill of St. Paul and Nobody Hill of Montevideo.

The suppression of difference among whites has had the paradoxical effect of accentuating it in poisonous ways. If we imagine that whites are homogeneous, then we are free to magnify the differences between whites and the rest of humanity; and we are also free either to glorify or to vilify white history but not to see it as merely one among many variations of the human story.

Manifest destiny and Western culture as the unique expression of patriarchal and racist rot are both readings of
history from the same point of view: both assume that
the Western story is in some unique way a radical departure from the human story.

I have recently been in the Platte River valley of
Nebraska. A man there took me to see his German
grandfather's homestead near Hastings in what is the
state's richest agricultural region. He showed me a
miles-long line of earth-sheltered bunkers, now crum-
bling like a prehistoric ruin. His grandfather's land,
the man told me, had been seized by the United States
government during World War II, along with that of
hundreds of other German immigrant farmers, and
turned into a vast ammunition depot. The farmers
themselves were conscripted into the military. The best
of their houses were moved to Hastings to make an officers' row; the rest were razed. Their families were left to
cope as best they could, as were the farmers who returned home from the war, heroes but landless. His
grandfather, my Nebraska guide told me, could never
drive past that depot without ranting and cursing. He
was bitter about it to his death.

There are many telling details in this story: that
good land was taken when any land might have done;
that the farmers displaced were Germans, surely not a
coincidence; that the government, just as in the hundreds of domestic treaties with Native-American nations,
was unilaterally breaking a promise; that after the war no
effort was made to restore either the land or the community; and that this took place in Nebraska not despite its
representatives in Washington but because one of them,
Senator George Norris, had used his unusual influence
to bring home a "development" plum.

But I am especially interested in a psychological detail with which the grandson now struggles. If it is true, as conventional wisdom currently has it, that white males are indiscriminately privileged in our culture, then how is this man to respond to what happened to his grandfather? There are only three possibilities, I think. One is to dismiss the grandfather as a weakling, somebody who could be stepped on and pushed around despite the advantages that society had offered him. The second is to appropriate his grandfather's rage and all that goes with it: a sense of malice against government, a declaration of fierce independence, and the bitter conviction that one will always, in the end, be taken. The third is to become a Good Boy, to atone for the grandfather's failure by taking the side of power. This third choice is the one the grandson seems to have made; he is now a veteran of both the Vietnam and Gulf wars and a devotee of military history, an enthusiasm his young son, he proudly reports, already shares.

His response is important because this is the story not just of a few German immigrants in the vicinity of Hastings, Nebraska nearly fifty years ago, but of the millions of farmers who have been forced from the land since the end of that war, always with the explanation that their work—their lives—were an impediment to the progress and prosperity of their society. If one were looking for the root causes of male violence in rural culture, this would seem to me a more revealing place to start than with the theories of patriarchal primacy that have such a hold on our imaginations.

None of the possibilities open to the grandson provides any psychological basis for community building. The first leads to the malaise of powerlessness, the second to the rejection of the authority of community, the

third away from the sense of local pride that is at the
heart of community. Struggle sometimes ennobles
people, but never debasement.

The point is that rural children have been educated
to believe that opportunity of every kind lies elsewhere
and that the last half century's rural experience of failure
and decline has been largely due to the incompetence,
or irrelevance, of rural people.

The substance of this analysis finally came home to
me as I listened to a lecture by a much honored geographer. He showed us a set of excellent slides recounting
the triumphal march of agriculture from its mean begin-
nings in Indian plots to its present glory, the three-crop,
cash-grain system, as he put it: corn, soybeans, and
Miami. I thought it was already a tired joke the first time
it was uttered, but the audience of rural schoolteachers
snickered politely. The geographer showed us maps of
corn belt townships from thirty years ago and from today.
The old maps were messy and cluttered, a jangle of property lines. The new ones were neat and orderly, rid of the
confusion of so many extraneous owners. Actually, the
geographer assured us, the lines on the map might look
even neater if one took into account the fact that the
modern operator—the embarrassing word "farmer" is
seldom used by such people—is as likely to rent land as
to own it: a nice advance in capital efficiency. He showed
us photographs of untidy old-time farm landscapes:
fencerows everywhere, and farmsteads with their
Victorian jumble of trees and houses and big old barns
and chicken coops and pig sheds and granaries. And
then he showed us photographs of nice modern farm
landscapes: no unsightly fences, no unproductive trees,
just big open fields of corn and soybeans stretching to
the horizon, and maybe somewhere in the distance one

nice farmstead with a row of evergreens, a ranch-style house, a sleek, corrugated-metal pole shed to house the equipment—something clean and efficient.

The geographer lingered at one particular photograph of a man unloading shell corn into a metal grain bin. He wanted us to appreciate the marvel of it. He pointed out the two tractors that were rigged with auger and elevator to carry the grain from the truck to the bin in one simple, efficient maneuver. He pointed out that there was only one person in the picture and five machines: an elevator, an auger, a truck, and two tractors. He counted them for us. "Think of it!" he said, beaming. "Thirty years ago there would have been four or five people in this picture and maybe only one machine! All that labor just to store a load of corn!" He paused to let us appreciate the scene. I felt as though we were expected to applaud, although nobody did.

The geographer used the word "efficient" like a mantra. That was the meaning of his story, he said: the rise of efficiency. When he was finished, I asked him to tell us what he meant by that word.

He looked confused, and he hesitated. Finally he said, "Well, I could be clever, I suppose, and make up some definition on the spot, but the truth is, I haven't really given it much thought."

I went home, seething with anger, and wrote him a sharp letter. If you're a scholar with any moral integrity, I wrote, you'll give some thought to what you mean by the words you celebrate.

A few days later came his reply. "Thank you for the emotion you have obviously invested in your letter," it said. "I regret, however, to say that I have made it a rule to respond only to rational correspondents."

I know another man who once served on the

governing board of the institution that employs the geographer. He is a farmer without a degree from any
school; he grew up in hard times and his parents needed
him at home. He's not in *Who's Who*, has never presided
over the meeting of any learned society, has never been
invited by any foreign government to give a lecture, and
has only one piece of writing to his name, a self-
published chapbook of sentimental poems entitled
"My Brother's Keeper."

I met him when I was the editor of the newspaper at
the institution he helped govern. He took the trouble to
get to know not only me but my parents, who were,
partly by choice, left out of the industrial revolution in
farming. They were among the people being weeded
out. But my friend the farmer-poet cared about them.
He stopped to see me every few weeks. Each time he
stopped, he inquired politely about the progress of my
newspaper and then asked me what I had published in it
lately that honored and protected the lives of my people.
I was never able to give him a satisfactory answer.

I left college and went on with my life. My parents
died. But my friend did not forget me or them. He still
telephones now and then or drops by for a visit. The last
time I saw him, he showed up in the middle of a blizzard.
He wanted to know, he said, what I was doing to honor
and protect the lives of my people. I gave him an answer,
but we both knew it was lame. I urged him to spend the
night with us. The storm was raging. He could not stay,
he said. He had to be at the hospital in the morning for
open-heart surgery.

I don't imagine that I need to tell you which man
strikes me as educated.

So here I am to do that man's bidding, to speak
against any economy that sees people as an expendable

resource, that draws balance sheets excluding from consideration the health of the communities on which they report, that defines as efficient any reduction in human labor no matter what its nonpecuniary consequences. Such an economy is not only bound eventually to fail. It is wrong.

Richard Lingemann, who wrote a history of small towns, calls our Midwestern villages disposable communities. He means that many of them did not emerge organically in places well suited to the development of towns. Rather, they were often merely real estate speculations or projects of the railroads, whose financial fortunes, in the end, prospered, whatever the fate of the towns they promoted. The geographer John C. Hudson found that more than half of the railroad towns in North Dakota, for example, were by 1984 "little more than neighborhood gathering points for local farmers, with perhaps a gasoline station, a store and post office, a tavern or two, plus one or more grain elevators. Most merchants in the towns disappeared so long ago that younger residents never knew their trade centers as anything but a collection of decaying buildings. But the railroad network remains today much as it did sixty-five years ago. . . . Railroad profits and losses never were tied closely to the economic fortunes of the towns they served, even less so in later years when everything except grain moved on the highway."

Our belief is, as Hudson puts it, that structure can be made to precede activity. This idea failed in the utopian communities of the nineteenth century, it failed in the disposable communities of the plains, it failed in the urban housing projects of the 1950s and 1960s, it failed in the New Towns of the 1970s, and yet it persists. How many thousands of industrial parks have been built along the edges of dying towns in recent decades, their empty streets cracking and heaving from freeze to freeze, their vacant lots sprouting pigweeds and cockleburs?

The idea that structure generates activity is a consequence of misapprehending technology, of regarding it not as a tool, but as an end in itself. Here are other examples of this idea at work in our culture: we can improve education by consolidating schools; we can make highways safer by designing them for higher speeds; we can solve urban blight by razing the neighborhoods that the poor live in and replacing them with more expensive units; we can reintegrate rural communities by installing fiber-optic links to the cities; we can reduce crime by building more prisons. The delusion in each of these instances is that individual or cultural behavior would change if only the right structure were in place.

The alternative is to think of entrepreneurial work as an option for our rural communities. I lived for fifteen happy years in Worthington, Minnesota, which bills itself as the Turkey Capital of the World. This is by now a sentimental label, since there is scarcely a turkey to be found in all of Nobles County. But the title once had some legitimacy. There was a thriving poultry industry at Worthington, fostered by two local hatchery men who enlisted the town's retailers and chamber of commerce in an ingenious promotion. Do your spring trade with us, they said to the region's farmers, and we'll give you a free chick for every dollar you spend. It was no gimmick. Everybody benefited: businesses saw more traffic, farmers received both the chicks and the income from the mature birds, and the poultry men eventually had a supply of turkeys and chickens for slaughter.

This scheme contributed to the establishment of the region around Worthington as an important national center of poultry production, a diversification that helped to pull the community through the dark years of the Great Depression. By the 1940s the town had begun to celebrate turkeys in an annual harvest festival, sponsored by local merchants as a way of thanking their rural patrons.

The festival, which included a parade of turkeys, musical and carnival entertainments, and moonlight dancing in the streets, was so great a success that presidential aspirants began to flock to it to make their big farm-policy speeches: Estes Kefauver; Adlai Stevenson; Richard Nixon; Hubert Humphrey, who liked to flatter the townsfolk by noting that the only election he ever lost was the one in which he skipped Turkey Day; Lyndon Johnson, who sulked because the sky dared to rain on him; and Robert Kennedy, who drew a cheering throng of 80,000, the largest crowd, no doubt, that Worthington will ever see.

But disease eventually thinned the flocks, and after the Second World War, as farms expanded, they also became more specialized. Turkeys in Nobles County were always a small-scale diversification, and with the coming of export-driven industrialization, farmers no longer felt they could afford to be distracted by them. Turkey farming at Worthington, Minnesota, gradually became a thing of the past.

A few years ago, the town, battered by yet another bust in the farm economy, began to dream about what it might do to build on the tradition that had fostered its turkey industry. After due deliberation a scheme was announced, but it was not a fresh alliance between farmers and merchants to cooperate for the benefit of all. The new scheme was to erect a gigantic fiberglass turkey at the edge of town to lure passersby off the interstate in the hope that they would drop a few bucks along the way. This, too, is part of the instruction we give our children.

What new work we make in the rural parts of our country these days is largely of the branch-manufacturing kind, assembling components or packing or canning: hard, monotonous, low paying. Rural Americans have attracted these jobs by selling themselves as cheap and undemanding and by putting up the cash to build the roads and sewers, construct the sewage treatment facilities, erect the buildings, and hire the additional police officers, court officials, and social workers that prove necessary in communities where people have neither satisfying work nor sufficient wages.

There are two ironies in these policies. First, our universities have recently discovered the evils of colonialism and are everywhere rewriting curricula to include this discovery, while simultaneously aiding and abeting the new colonialism of the countryside. The geographer I mentioned, for example, has recently published a paper in which he disputes, on the basis of some of his graduate students' work, the prevailing perception that small rural towns are dying. It may be true, he says, that many rural towns have lost their retail centers, but they have at the same time gained a host of manufacturing plants. The gains might be even greater, he observes—in the circumspect language of scholarship, of course—if rural towns weren't hampered by retrograde leaders unable to stomach change and get on with the program for progress. To me, there is a vast difference between entrepreneurial farming in a community that offers a full range of services and amenities and factory work eviscerating chickens under conditions that guarantee you carpal tunnel syndrome, for $6.50 an hour, in a town where you can't buy a decent pair of shoes. The difference, to me, bears little resemblance to progress.

In any case, I hate that deceitful shibboleth about change, a favorite of social planners and progressive ministers. American farmers have been as receptive to technological change as any group in our society. They have come, in half a century, from horse power and a set of techniques essentially constant for more than a millennium to computers and bioengineering. Most of them have, in fact, changed themselves right out of existence. The pietists of change are those who would like to see more of the same. When one suggests that there may be better alternatives, they say, "Ah! There you go again, wallowing in the myths of the past!" We cannot change present policy, in other words, because to do so would be to resist change. It is not exactly a watertight argument, but it carries the day with depressing regularity.

The second irony is that, while industrialization has been sold as an escape from the hard labor of farming, it has brought an even harder and meaner kind of work, and at less potential for financial gain.

These are lessons we teach our rural children today: that their parents were expendable and that their duty is to abandon their dreams and to become cogs in the industrial machine.

Here is another message we give them, in ways both subtle and direct: if they expect to amount to anything, they had better leave home. The truth is, the future we are preparing for ourselves in rural America does not include a place for ambitious young men and women. A friend of mine who teaches at a rural university says that the institution ought frankly to offer a class called "How to Migrate."

When we sell ourselves, in the name of economic

development, as ideally suited to the least attractive kinds of factory work because our people are willing to labor hard and at subsistence wages without complaining or organizing, or when we allow the rest of society to dump its toxic trash in our land because we'll do anything for a few jobs, what are we telling our children about our ideals, our hopes and dreams?

Sometimes the message is more subtle: We are constantly putting down the professional person who chooses to work among us as less competent than the folks who have made it in the big cities. My wife's practice as a small-town defense attorney is an example. One night, when she was out for a meeting, the telephone rang. The caller was another professional woman in town, a friend. She was looking for Nancy. I said that she wasn't in. "Well," our friend said, "perhaps you can help me. That boy who's been charged with attempted murder — some of us are certain he's innocent. We're organizing a defense fund for him, and we need to hire an attorney."

"I'm not the lawyer," I said, "but Nancy will be back any minute, and I'm sure she'd be glad to help."

"You understand, of course," she replied, "how serious this charge is. We need to hire a real attorney, somebody from the Twin Cities."

She said it without the slightest intention, I'm sure, of putting my wife down. It's just an assumption we make: if you were any good, you wouldn't be here. What does that assumption, which is everywhere in the rural air, say to our children?

*If you're any good, you go somewhere else. You go where good people go.* We raise our most capable rural children from the beginning to expect that as soon as possible they will leave and that if they are at all successful, they will never return. We impose upon them, in effect, a kind of homelessness. The work of reviving rural communities will begin when we can imagine a rural future that makes a place for at least some of our best and brightest children, when they are welcome to be at home among us. Only then will we be serious about any future at all.

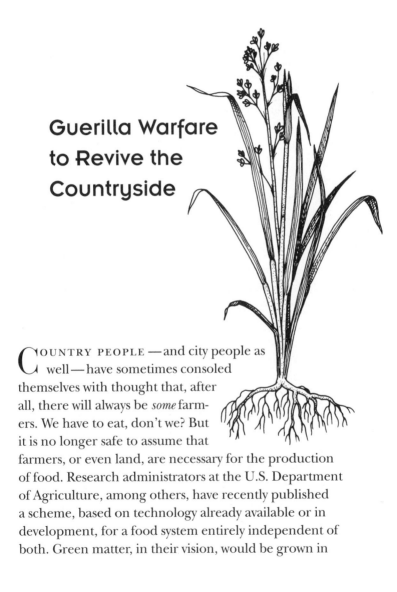

# Guerilla Warfare
# to Revive the
# Countryside

COUNTRY PEOPLE —and city people as
well—have sometimes consoled
themselves with thought that, after
all, there will always be *some* farmers. We have to eat, don't we? But
it is no longer safe to assume that
farmers, or even land, are necessary for the production
of food. Research administrators at the U.S. Department
of Agriculture, among others, have recently published
a scheme, based on technology already available or in
development, for a food system entirely independent of
both. Green matter, in their vision, would be grown in

factory tanks in solutions of water and various chemicals; this organic material would be reduced by enzymes to syrups in other factories; the syrups would be reconstituted in still other factories — artificially flavored, colored, and formed as necessary—to resemble old-fashioned strawberries, or broccoli, or beefsteaks, or whatever.

One of the difficulties in industrializing agriculture has been the unsuitability of the farm to the assembly-line model. Most farms yield only a single crop a year and, even when gestation cycles make more than one generation of livestock a year possible, the gestation itself cannot much be hurried. Despite synthetic fertilizers, irrigation, and a medicine bag full of herbicides, insecticides, fungicides, and antibiotics, farming in nature remains frustratingly susceptible to its vagaries: variable growing seasons, unpredictable rainfalls, violent storms, explosions of disease, the genetic mutability of pests, the structural characteristics of soil. Yields, too, are always somewhat unpredictable, and most natural, unprocessed foods have short shelf lives, making effective management of agricultural inventories stubbornly difficult. Consumer resistance has been growing as well: those crops best suited to the long-distance hauling and frequent handling of the modern food system are often not the best tasting or most nutritious.

If we could bring farming out of the fields and into the factories, these obstacles might be managed. We would then have an authentically industrial farming system. Farming could be run around the clock and around the year in an artifical and sterile enviroment where weather and other unpredictables could be accelerated or slowed to accomodate changes in demand and concocted like infant formulas to uniform standards of taste and nutrition. Best of all, such a regimen would not require the services of a single independent farmer; the system would be firmly within the control of a few giant corporations. Farming would then be, by the labor productivity measure with which we have been preoccupied, perfectly efficient.

The proponents of this scheme were miffed when their description of it as a form of sustainable agriculture was met with some derision. They were right to be miffed: if one thinks of agriculture as only another industrial process, as they have, then this vision of the future is not only logical but inevitable.

Think of what industrialization has already brought to agriculture: a reduction of the farm workforce from 50 percent of the population to less than 2 percent of it; a 23 percent reduction in the farmer's share of the American agricultural dollar, in constant dollar terms, since 1910, while at the same time input costs have quintupled, and the marketing and processing share of the agricultural dollar has increased nearly six-and-a-half times to about two-thirds of the total; and the development of a handful of huge, vertically integrated agribusiness corporations that operate in many segments of the American agricultural economy—most notably in meat production, processing, and marketing—essentially without economic competition. Half of all the fed beef in this country, to take one example, is now produced by four corporations on twenty feedlots.

American farmers survive essentially at the mercy of their suppliers and buyers. There is no reason to suppose, if there is a way to produce food and fiber without land or farmers, that such mercy will be long suffering.

Neither is there reason to suppose that national policy can effectively mitigate the power that the increasingly transnational agribusiness giants now wield.

The biggest of them are already in a position to play nations against each other to the detriment of the public interest, just as industrial interests have played states and cities against one another to keep taxes, wages, and worker benefits low and to limit environmental and workplace regulations.

To propose in the conventional way that some combination of reforms of the current system can be devised to save rural communities is, I believe, to tilt at windmills. The system as it is has become well entrenched, politically powerful, and, for some, lucrative: in the industrial sector of our economy, only the drug companies have higher net returns than the food processors. The industrialists are organized, visible, and well capitalized. Rural communities are in disarray after decades of loss and retrenchment, largely invisible, and poor.

The rural poor are, moreover, the wrong kind of poor to attract political attention: they are largely white, they are employed, and many of them continue to live in what we have come to call, perhaps inadvisedly, traditional families. They defy our stereotypes about who is abused by our economic system. Our stereotypes are founded upon the prevailing notion that power and wealth are distributed in our society primarily by race and gender, an analysis that significantly obscures the still powerful factor of class.

We have also, I think, mistakenly made the "family farm" the moral focus of our case for agricultural reform. In the days when a majority of the nation's population lived on subsistence farms, this claim carried some genuine weight; to do what was right for family farms in those times really did amount to doing something that was also economically and socially just. But now, when the richest person in a rural town is likely to be a "family farmer" and

when the laws of the land permit a corporate giant like
Tyson Foods, for tax and welfare purposes, to register
itself as a family farm, the term has lost useful meaning.
We have arrived at the paradoxical point where any
general measure to benefit family farms, as they are
currently defined, will serve only to increase the compete-
tive advantage and further enrich those citizens in rural
communities who are already at the top of the heap.

Moral arguments carry persuasive weight to the
extent that they appeal to the good of the whole community. The task in moral terms is not to benefit farmers but
to benefit society as a whole. The strongest moral argument against our present system of agriculture is not that
it hurts individual farmers—although it does—but that
it tends toward totalitarianism: the system concentrates
wealth and power to the disadvantage of most citizens,
urban as well as rural, and does so at an accelerating
pace. In a food system increasingly dominated, as ours is,
by transnational conglomerates with economic monopo-
lies, urban consumers have fewer meaningful choices
about what they will eat and whom they will support with
their food dollars; rural producers have fewer choices
about what they will grow, how it will be grown, and where
it will be marketed; and urban and rural communities
alike lose power to influence businesses to make deci-
sions that work to the general social, environmental, and
economic good. The work of reform, therefore, is to
think in terms of devising a system of food production
that expands the possibilities for choice at every level and
for every member of the community and not simply to
think in terms of the economic needs of some producers.

My sense is that such an alternative will be accomplished not by a frontal assault on the existing system but
only by creating an alternative that renders it irrelevant

and obsolete. I have in mind a kind of guerrilla warfare — the classic tactic of the underpowered — in which the actions are economic and communitarian rather than military. To this end, I offer the following as ideas for getting started:

1.  We can plan. On many farms, the only serious planning is for the current season's crops; and in many small towns, economic-development planning means laying some sewer in an empty field at the edge of town, putting up a sign along the highway that says *Mudville: A Friendly Place To Grow,* and sending off one of the old boys to a nearby city to look for a manufacturer thinking about expansion — *if* it can get twenty years of tax breaks, subsidized utility rates, maybe a free building, and a ready supply of workers who would rather die than join a union and who are hungry enough to work at subsistence wages. Cargill has a carefully considered long-range plan and a clear set of ideas about how to get there. An alternative — one that does not callously set up American farmers against foreign farmers to their mutual destruction, as Cargill does — cannot be constructed without the same kind of consideration. The best ideas I've seen about planning for farmers that might work for communities, too, are in Allan Savory's *Holistic Resource Management.* Savory's approach to planning begins with the real bottom-line question, "What kind of life do you want?" rather than with the conventional question, "How much money do you want?" to which the only honest answer is, "More."
2.  We can learn to think locally. In the town where I now live, several main-street buildings have recently become vacant. The local chamber of commerce's

approach to this problem is typical—to launch a search for chain retail outlets to fill the gaps. What if the vacancies were seen, instead, as opportunities to set up local young people in businesses of their own? What if the money that is being spent on seeking absentee owners were invested in owners with a long-term commitment to the community, people who would spend their profits locally, send their children to the local schools, and take a personal interest in the vitality of the community? One problem in colonies—which small rural towns have become— is that the capital, both human and monetary, is constantly being siphoned from them into the bigger and wealthier communities where the colonial entrepreneurs live.

Perhaps, at the same time, if we were not so xenophobic, we could find ways to reverse the flow of human capital. Our great cities all have significant populations of homeless people, while the countryside is dotted with cheap, empty houses. And many urban people dream of escaping the crime, filth, and overpopulation of large cities. What if we were to concentrate economic-development resources on finding entrepreneurial opportunities for such people in our small towns? They could bring to us not only their economic skills but fresh points of view and a new enthusiasm for small-town life that would revitalize our own energies and rekindle our own ambitions.

3. We can create local information systems. The existing information systems—chiefly, in small towns, the land grant Extension Service and the chamber of commerce—are wedded—although within the Extension Service there are encouraging signs of

change — to the economic system already in place. A sound alternative to it will not be built on their advice, so rural people will have to sponsor their own farm- and community-based research programs, organize their own seminars, start their own study circles, and create their own support systems. The Land Stewardship Project in Minnesota offers a model for such self-education.

4. While a new economic system is being built in the countryside, we must continue to challenge vigorously the existing one, not because we expect to defeat it but because we need to make a space in which our own ideas can grow and because the resources our enemies spend in defending themselves are resources that they cannot deploy against us. Such an attack would oblige rural people to maintain an active interest in politics, one that moves considerably beyond narrow and immediate self-interest. Alloca-tion of research dollars, trade policies, technology policy, and economic-development policy all, for example, have far-reaching consequences for rural America, but only when the issue is something like commodity prices or disaster relief are the voices of rural Americans now heard loudly and clearly in the political system.

5. Now that the cooperatives of an earlier era have become, mostly, too big to fulfill their original purposes, it is time to reinvent them: neighborhood equipment cooperatives that will help young people get started in farming; purchasing cooperatives that will give small-town retailers a fighting chance against the chain merchants on the outskirts of town; consumer cooperatives that give small-towners access to goods and services otherwise unavailable in

the countryside; land cooperatives, perhaps, as an alternative to absentee ownership; production cooperatives that keep some of the processing and distribution dollars in the countryside.

6. Farmers found ways during the economic crisis of the early 1980s to reduce significantly their consumption of purchased inputs—artificial fertilizers, animal drugs, pesticides, new machinery, and the like. The gains that were made then need to be consolidated, and a new push needs to be made to reduce farmers' dependency on imported supplies.

7. Growing as much food as we can locally will result not only in fresher and tastier food but also in more diverse and healthier local economies. Such results will be accomplished only as farmers bypass the existing marketing system and re-establish their own direct links with consumers. Even in the forbidding climate of the northern plains, eggs, meat, some kinds of fresh fish, root crops, squashes, berries, cheeses, milk, honey, and summertime supplies of greens, legumes, some fruits, and many standard vegetables could be produced within twenty miles of their consumers. Perhaps it is not outrageous to imagine the revival of the local grain mills and breweries that were a standard feature of pre-industrial rural communities.

One model that is catching on in some parts of the country is the CSA, shorthand for Community Supported Agriculture. I belong to a CSA myself. For a fee paid in advance, a local farm family provides me with a large shopping bag full of fresh produce every week during the growing season, sometimes with a bouquet of flowers; some of these cooperatives also supply their members with honey, cheeses, eggs, and fresh meat. The farmer gets in return a reliable market and an interest-free advance on his production costs. Both parties benefit from the bonus of getting to know one another and other members, as well as opportunities to join in the farm work, newsletters, and parties; it is an exercise in community building as much as in food production. Indeed, the scheme does not seem to work when the only benefit being offered is food.

Community-minded institutions in small towns could support this effort—independent schools, colleges, hospitals, and nursing homes, for example —by contracting in the same way with local farmers for those supplies that can practicably be raised locally. And if the idea catches on, we might even begin again to produce some of our own clothing, to manufacture some of our own furniture, and to provide some of our own entertainment.

8. One obstacle to local food production is a regulatory structure that was intended to guarantee the safety of our food but which operates now, in many instances, only to protect industrial food processors from local competition. My sister, who lives in a small rural town with a rich Scandanavian heritage, developed a cottage industry around the making of *lefse* for holiday parties during the Christmas season. She did all of the work herself in her own kitchen, and because it was excellent *lefse,* she soon gained a devoted clientele. She came to depend on that little business to finance her Christmas gift-giving. But one day the local food inspector got wind of her business and ordered her to shut down until she could install an industrial kitchen, which she could not afford to do. She was suddenly out of business,

although the safety of the food she was providing
was never in question. The rules need to be rewrit-
ten to prevent harassment of cottage industries—
which have not, after all, produced the eggs we dare
not eat raw or poultry routinely carrying salmonella
or hamburgers contaminated with E. coli, or fruits
bathed in pesticide residues, dyed to make them
look ripe, and waxed to make them glisten.

9. We could fully value the work of women. Women's
   suffrage began in the rural West. Let economic
   equality for women begin in the countryside, too.
   This will only happen, I think, as women themselves
   join together in entrepreneurial partnerships, analyz-
   ing local economies for open niches in markets,
   organizing revolving loan funds that bypass unimagi-
   native banks, selling local institutions—schools,
   churches, hospitals, nursing homes—on the virtues
   of locally-supplied goods and services, and taking
   heart and instruction from the economic awaken-
   ing that Third World women are beginning to
   experience.

10. We could embrace the new generation of immigrants
    to the countryside—the Latinos and Asians attracted
    by jobs in the food-processing plants—as an asset
    rather than a problem. We could celebrate the cul-
    tural diversity that they bring to our communities by
    welcoming the fresh energy and imagination that
    they carry with them, making entrepreneurial oppor-
    tunities for them, and inviting them into positions of
    leadership. We could spice our mundane lives with
    new languages, new customs, new foods, new music,
    and new ways of dancing.

11. We could begin to restore the ecological fabric
    of the countryside. We could make our towns and

villages into gardens rather than setting them, as we do now, in sterile, suburban lawns. Let the children in every school restore a portion of their school grounds to native vegetation. Let our roadsides blossom again with wildflowers. Let our livestock farmers rediscover the virtues in pastures. Let us reserve a greenway along every lake and pond, every creek and river in the countryside. Over the last fifty years we have made of the countryside an industrial landscape that is, like all industrial landscapes, ugly. Were we to make the countryside beautiful again and safe for wild creatures, perhaps more people would want to join us in living there.

12. We could teach our children rural history and rural culture. We could introduce them to the artists of the countryside. We could raise them to know the ecological and geological history of the place to which they have been born. We could celebrate and practice the distinctiveness of rural culture rather than settling for the mass culture of the TV screen and the Wal-Mart. Perhaps if we gave these gifts to our children, and if we provided them with ways to earn more than a subsistence living, at least some of our children might be content to make their lives among us.

3

# Steady
# Growth

SUPPOSE EVERYTHING grew at
the rate of five percent a year.

If I fulfilled my actuarial ex-
pectancy, I would weigh, at death,
about 740 pounds, having spent
the last eight or ten years of my
life in bed or in a specially con-
structed wheelchair, dependent upon caretakers still
young and slender enough to be ambulatory. Perhaps, by
then, human beings would have taken to the buoyant
water like whales or hippopotamuses.

We would be safe there from the monster insects
roaming the land.

In the mountains, thirty years from now, 1600-pound grizzlies would roam the high meadows, preying upon rabbit-sized pikas, dog-sized marmots, and an occasional obese sightseer.

The hackberries in my yard would be fifteen stories high. In California sequoias would be as tall as the Empire State Building, and apartment complexes could be excavated in them, saving the expense of sawmilling and preserving the habitat for owls.

Tourists would flock in their specially built vans to the Lamar Valley of Yellowstone National Park to see the majestic two-ton buffaloes and Old Faithful shooting spumes of hot water sixty-five stories into the air.

Suppose that we increased the size of everything we owned by five percent a year.

Soon even the poorest of our citizens would live in houses the size of the tract mansions that are popping up like mushrooms in the suburbs of our burgeoning cities, and every rich person would own a palace like Versailles.

We would drive around, thirty years hence, in sixty-five-foot-long cars powered by small nuclear reactors. We could store the spent fuel in repositories in inner-city neighborhoods, or in the most decrepit rural ones.

We would sit in high chairs at our seven-foot-tall tables, manipulating the gigantic tableware to our mouths with the aid of an arrangement of pulleys and levers. When we had finished eating, we would be wheeled to bathrooms where a system of pneumatic tubes in the floor would raise us to towering sinks to wash our faces, and then to our beds, into which we would be deposited by small elevators.

Books would be beyond us. They would all weigh thirty pounds or more and have individual words in them that took up whole pages, and in any case, we would have agreed that the meanings in books are too indeterminate to be appreciated by anybody without a Ph.D. in one of the more exotic branches of literary theory. We would spend our time watching seven-hour-long cartoon romances on sixteen-foot square TV screens.

In the land grant universities, the biotechnologists, after years of experimentation with growth hormones, would finally arrive at the ideal—one gigantic cow to supply the nation's milk; one or two pigs the size of New York City maturing on schedule every three months to fulfill the demand for the other white meat; one turkey a year with breasts the size of Iowa and an IQ of zero to satisfy the Thanksgiving trade; and in the middle of the country, a thousand-mile square cornfield, tilled by a single farmer running a tractor twenty stories high and pulling two-thousand-row equipment through the tree-sized plants to supply our industrial output.

After all, why shouldn't we expect nature to perform like the economy?

# Naming
# What
# We Love

ESTABLISHING a relationship with
nature—or with anything else,
for that matter—is not a matter of
networking. It is not a hobby, like
collecting a life list of birds, nor is
it something one catches through
casual contact, by camping out on vaca-
tions, for example. A healthy relationship is ongoing,
persistent, and resilient despite boredom, disappoint-
ments, adversities, infidelities. It is defined by its dailiness, a dailiness expressed in two dimensions—as a
labor and as a need.

As a labor: not so much the labor of sweat and tears, although that too, but more the labor of attentiveness, of being present, of receptivity, of abiding, as Wendell Berry has said, "like water, which fills the place it comes to/ until a way is found."

As a need: The Old English antecedent of *need* suggests an imperative that is emotionally felt as well as practical, unlike the Latinate *necessity*, which is formal, objective, impersonal. Water is a necessity; love is a need.

One way to understand our relationship with nature is to undertake the basic work of naming its constituents. The last great age of naming began in the Enlightenment and ended with the close of the Victorian era. The time was the heyday of natural history, when eccentric gentlemen of means, Charles Darwin among them, and destitute but resourceful swashbucklers, as often as not scientifically untrained, roamed the world in search of adventure and exotica. What they discovered laid the foundations for revolutions in both biology and geology, and these revolutions, in turn, profoundly altered our present perceptions of life and nature.

Natural history, once the domain of the namers, is these days a musty calling for those who keep alive its literary, not its scientific, tradition. Writers of natural history as diverse in their temperaments and methods as Annie Dillard and Edward Abbey, while grounding their works in close readings of modern science and of nature, have insisted that they are not natural historians and should not be read as such. Natural history now seems amateurish, dilettantish, not quite grown-up, decidedly old-fashioned.

Science, for its part, has become a priesthood. Its meticulously trained practitioners are suitably cloistered

in academies or corporate research laboratories. They
speak a language, for the most part, that even well-
educated persons outside their specialties cannot understand, communicating through journals and the
proceedings of societies impenetrable to the general
public. The problems they address are often technical
and specialized.

Natural historians have become outmoded and sci-
entists isolated at precisely that moment in our history
when we fear that our very lives may depend upon how
well we understand nature and our own responsibilities
and limits within it. Bill McKibben, in *The End of Nature*,
proclaimed nature itself dead, or at death's door. I do not
take this pronouncement literally. While I believe that it
has never been more within the realm of possibility that
we might doom the life of our own species, I cannot yet
believe — perhaps this is a baseless optimism — that we
are clever enough or powerful enough to defeat life itself.
Nevertheless, there is a way in which, for all practical purposes, we render nature meaningless to humanity, at our
own peril: we have faltered in the naming process.

We are justly proud of all that we have learned in
the past five thousand years or so of literate life. We have
peered into the mysterious universe of the atom, learned
to unravel and read the genetic code, manufactured new
forms of life. We have counted the stars in the Milky Way
and the galaxies in the universe. But we do not yet know,
even to the nearest order of magnitude, the number of
kinds of life on earth. The only thing, in fact, that we do
know with any confidence is that the majority of the
earth's species remain to be discovered, much less
named. There are some whole living systems on earth —
the soil ecosystems, for example, upon which we are utterly dependent for our sustenance — that remain almost

as hidden to us as the galaxies beyond our own. Perhaps ninety-five percent of the organisms living in soils have yet to be identified.

It is true that we have named more of the earth's living things now than ever before, which would seem to be making headway. At the same time, under our influence the earth is experiencing its greatest rate of species extinction in at least tens of millions of years, and the rate has the potential to reach unprecedented proportions. Our net effect, then, is one of destroying, and thereby rendering forever nameless, more information about life on earth than we are gaining.

And we have sufficiently altered the earth's atmosphere and irreversibly set into motion a warming of the world's climate. This warming is likely to outpace the rate at which adapted plants can move across the landscape. What consequences this will bear for the diversity and distribution of life on earth we cannot predict.

At the local level there is a growing illiteracy about the natural world, paradoxical as that might seem, given the nearly universal anxiety we feel about the state of our environment. I first began to think about this problem when, in a review of a book I had much admired, a critic said, "This writer knows the names of more plants than anyone else I know." This comment excited my attention because I had failed to notice that quality in the book. So I went back to the text and counted. I found, in all, the names of thirteen plants of the commonest household varieties: petunias, roses, lilacs, and the like. Can the reviewer be serious? I wondered, and then I thought, sadly, that he probably was.

Recently, at the instigation of a neighbor, I have had a visit from my town's weed inspector. The condition of my yard, in which grow some plants with no close

relationship to Kentucky bluegrass, has been a terrible
aggravation to this neighbor. His first protest was polite
enough—a gift of promotional literature from the local
ChemLawn franchise. Then he telephoned to ask that I
cut down a number of shrubs and a tree that is dead. I
removed the shrubs but balked at cutting the tree, ex-
plaining that I welcome the birds it attracts. He escalated
the attack by removing the branches of the trees on his
side of our common property line and dumping them in
my yard. When this provoked no response, he complained
about the condition of my yard to the weed inspector.

The weed inspector sent me a registered letter. I
was the subject, it informed me, of a citizen complaint
and had five days to remove the offending vegetation
(unspecified) or the city would move in and mow,
spray, bulldoze, or take whatever other action was
necessary—bombing not explicitly excluded—to do
so, with expenses borne by me.

I telephoned the weed inspector. "Can you tell me,"
I asked, "what in particular you object to about my yard?"
Well, no, he couldn't, he said. He had never seen it. I
invited him over for an inspection and asked him to
identify the problem plants for me. He came and wandered aimlessly about, finally halting in front of a catnip
plant. He kicked at it with his boot. "Well, what about
this?" he said. "This doesn't look like the sort of thing
that ought to be growing here."

"Can you tell me what it is?" I asked.

"I'd have to look it up," he said. "And what about
that?" he said, poking at a wild phlox. "That looks like the
sort of thing I see in places that haven't been kept up."

"What is it?"

"Well what about *this*?" he said, stabbing at a
meadow rue.

The scene repeated itself several times.

"I don't have time to run around looking every little thing up in the books!" he finally huffed.

Then, after getting hold of himself, his tone turned friendly and confidential. "If I were you, I'd just cut them all down. You'll make a lot of trouble, you know, if you don't."

He paused. "Do *you* know what they are?"

"Yes," I said, "and I don't mind making a little trouble, if it comes to that."

He stared at me hard, shrugged his shoulders, and went away muttering under his breath. I felt relieved but also distressed at having, in my modest attempt to make room for nature in my own yard, aroused so much anguish in my neighbor, whom I enjoyed and would have liked to please. We lived so near and yet in such distant worlds.

More recently I took two groups of the brightest seniors in our high school — sixty of them in all — on a walk along the lake that most of them have frequented since they were infants. When we had walked a bit, I stopped and asked them to name as many of the plants as they could. A few of the students could name a handful; they were mostly farm kids who knew the weeds. But the majority of the students could name no more than two or three. The dandelion was the only plant they all knew. They didn't recognize cattails. Most of them couldn't tell the difference between a willow tree and a cottonwood tree. They have wandered and played along that lakeshore for a lifetime, utterly blind to it.

We are fond of saying that we are living in an information explosion, but in some critical respects this statement is an absolute delusion. No group of Santee youths, standing on the shore of Lake Okabena two hundred years ago, would have been ignorant of its natural life or devoid of language to describe its landscape. No Santee child would have been unaware of the connections between the health of the earth and the health of human life. I think no farm child living seventy-five years ago, or fifty years ago, would have been quite so innocent of these matters either. I am not convinced that we are experiencing an explosion of understanding. On the contrary, just as every species extinction deprives us of certain volumes of information, obtainable, even if unread, so the general decline of intimate relationships with the natural world, and therefore of our knowledge of nature, has left us bereft of information that no marvel of biotechnological engineering, however sophisticated or clever, can possibly restore or replace.

Something of the same confusion now reigns even within the biological sciences. Twenty-five years ago, we were able to say with some confidence that we understood, at least in general terms, what an ecosystem was and how it moved, through a series of successions, toward a complex but stable climax. But the recent work of mathematically inclined specialists, particularly the population biologists, calls into debate if not outright question even this basic perception of nature. Similarly, chaos mathematicians have recently taught us to see that the behavior of the physical world is vastly more complex and difficult to predict than we once thought and that even very tiny disturbances in the world can have enormous and quite unexpected effects. This new understanding is popularly epitomized in meteorologist Edward Lorenz's famous "Butterfly Effect," the proposition that the flapping of a butterfly's wings in Beijing can ultimately influence the storm patterns over New York or Minneapolis.

We are less certain now than at any time in this century that we can accurately perceive any prevailing sense of order in the natural world. Some of us are inclined to think that there is no order, that change and disturbance rule the world. Others—myself among them—are inclined to believe that we have simply reached a plateau in our learning; that, as at many other junctures in history, we have seen enough to invalidate our prevailing picture of the world but not yet enough to make a satisfying new picture.

A very old but not outmoded idea is that we will find our salvation in what we love. We have learned in recent times to fear for the earth, for its suddenly apparent fragility, and for all that we obviously do not know about it. But fear is no basis for an intelligent relationship; ignorance and indulgence preempt the love that is required of us. We will love the earth more competently, more effectively, by being able to name and know something about the life it sustains.

Can you, I asked those students, imagine a satisfactory love relationship with someone whose name you do not know? I can't. It is perhaps the quintessentially human characteristic that we cannot know or love what we have not named. Names are passwords to our hearts, and it is there, in the end, that we will find the room for a whole world.

## Discovering
## One's Own Place

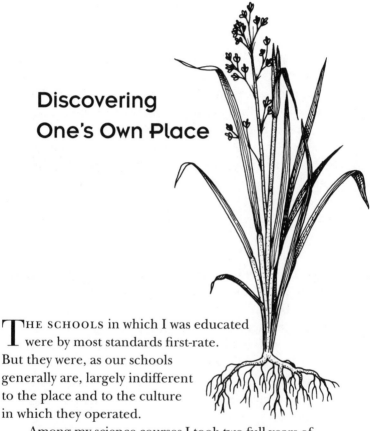

T HE SCHOOLS in which I was educated
were by most standards first-rate.
But they were, as our schools
generally are, largely indifferent
to the place and to the culture
in which they operated.

Among my science courses I took two full years of
biology, but I never learned that the beautiful meadow
at the bottom of my family's pasture was remnant virgin
prairie. We did not spend, so far as I can remember, a
single hour on prairies—the landscape in which we
were immersed—in two years of biological study.

I took history courses for years, but I never learned that one of the founders of my town and for decades its leading banker—the man who platted the town and organized its school system, its library, its parks, and its fire department—was also the author of the first comprehensive treatise on Minnesota's prairie botany. I can only imagine now what it might have meant to me—a studious boy with a love of nature—to know that a great scholar of natural history had made a full and satisfying life in my town. I did not know until long after I left the place that it afforded the possibility of an intellectual life.

I read, in the course of twelve years of English instruction, many useful and stimulating books, but I never learned that someone who had won a National Book Award for poetry—Robert Bly—was living and working on a farm only thirty miles from our house. The countryside was full of writers, I would later discover, but I did not meet anybody who had written a book until I went away to college. I had not imagined, or been encouraged to imagine, that it was possible to live in the country and to write books, too. Nor did I suspect that it was possible to write books about *our* countryside. We read Sir Walter Scott, John Steinbeck, and Robert Frost, but not O.E. Rolvaag or Black Elk, Lois Hudson or Thomas McGrath, Meridel LeSueur or Frederick Manfred. We did not read them at the University of Minnesota, either. I was left to unearth by my own devices, years later, the whole fine literature of my place.

I took a six-quarter survey of Western thought at the University of Minnesota in which the only nature that came up for consideration was human nature. When we got to the Americans, we skipped right over Whitman and Melville, Emerson and Thoreau, and got down, first thing, to T.S. Eliot and Henry James. The great writers, I learned, were not rural and were not interested in nature; in the American instance, they were even expatriate.

I studied industrial arts with a man who taught me how to make a wooden nightstand and an electric motor; I did not learn until many years later that on his own time he made wonderful lithographs and woodblock prints of the prairie landscape. I grew up believing that scenery consisted of mountains and waterfalls and deer, and that there was nothing worth seeing in our own tedious flatlands.

I studied vocational agriculture. I learned how to identify thirty common weeds and how to formulate a good pig ration, but nothing of the history of farming and nothing that might have encouraged me to think critically about how we farm. My father was an organic farmer. What I mainly learned from my vocational agriculture classes was that he was a nut.

Nothing in my education prepared me to believe, or encouraged me to expect, that there was any reason to be interested in my own place. If I hoped to amount to anything, I understood, I had better take the first road east out of town as fast as I could. And, like so many of my classmates, I did.

Here is a symptom of the thinness with which we have settled rural America: we have made communities that we have always in some sense thought of as disposable. Many of the first white towns of the Midwest were established by speculators, either railroad companies or individual opportunists: in the case of the railroads as the efficient collectors of farm commodities, in the case of individuals as short-term real estate ventures. Our towns were planned, by and large, as profit centers, not as communities. They flourished for two or three decades and, by the 1920s, when both the psychic and the economic energy of the nation had begun to flow from the countryside into the great cities, they were already starting to fail.

We said then, as we do now, that those who fought to preserve the vitality of rural towns were victims of nostalgia, unable or unwilling to keep up with the times. We still have not noticed that the phrase "bedroom community," a place merely to sleep, is an oxymoron: a community is by definition a population with a common interest distinct from that of the larger world; it is a place with more than convenience at its heart; it has some shared work to do; and it has a shared history. If one follows the word *community* to its Latin root, one finds that it literally means a group of people who have made together the rite of passage from adolescence into adulthood.

Here is another symptom: we have occupied this continent now for four centuries, but with the exception of the sunflower we have yet to make significant use of any of its thousands of native plants as a source of food. Ninety-five percent of our nutrition comes from thirty plants, all of them originating in what we call the Third World. That we have made so little use of our land's biotic wealth is a striking measure of how little we have settled into it. Ironically, even the weeds that plague our imported crops have been imported. When we came here, we packed up even our troubles and brought them along.

Here is yet another symptom: only about one-tenth of one percent of the native tallgrass prairie that covered the central United States at the time of white settlement remains. The tallgrass prairie region was once exactly comparable in size to the Amazon rain basin, now similarly threatened. Although we have squandered half the topsoil that lay beneath its virgin sod in our first century of farming, it remains the richest agricultural land on the planet. Had we had any appreciation for the place we were appropriating, had we been thinking from the beginning in terms of making real homes here, we would have felt compelled to preserve at least representative samples of the land we found for the future. We might even have imagined, as we have yet to do, that the life that was prospering here when we arrived might have had some instruction to offer us about how to succeed in this strange new world.

# What Time Is It?

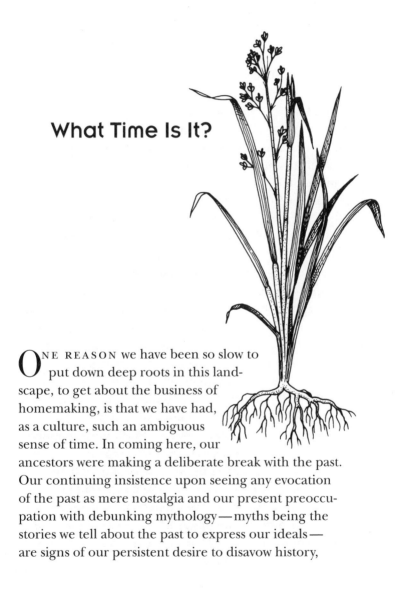

O NE REASON we have been so slow to
put down deep roots in this landscape, to get about the business of
homemaking, is that we have had,
as a culture, such an ambiguous
sense of time. In coming here, our
ancestors were making a deliberate break with the past.
Our continuing insistence upon seeing any evocation
of the past as mere nostalgia and our present preoccu-
pation with debunking mythology — myths being the
stories we tell about the past to express our ideals —
are signs of our persistent desire to disavow history,

to imagine that we could make a new culture free of the baggage of our origins. At the same time, we continually regard the present as profoundly corrupted, as not at all what we intended. Dismissing past and present, we have been cornered into a blind faith in the future. Change, any kind and at any cost, has been our creed, our aimless hope. When one is adrift in a relentless current, one does not think of putting down roots.

Quite recently, however, even the future has come under doubt, as our conceptions of time further erode. We have had two good ideas about time, one already abandoned, and the other well on its way to the same fate. Our first idea was that time is cyclical, that nothing fundamental ever changes, that as the days come and go into seasons and years, each identical in pattern to the last, so history endlessly turns back upon itself. More recently we have thought of time as progressive, moving both steadfastly forward, relentless and unstoppable, and upward, carrying with it, especially, the advances of the human species in knowledge, sophistication, and civility. Two insights have caused us to doubt this second idea of time: first is relativity, the understanding of time as a coordinate in space, and, therefore, plastic; and second is the perception that what has looked all along like progress might in fact be a march in the wrong direction. We suddenly see that our intelligence has as much chance of destroying us as of lifting us into glory.

For the moment, then, our sense of time is in limbo. Just as we have lost a clear sense of how the universe works—until quite recently, we were confident that it worked like a clock—so we have lost a coherent picture of time. If it does not move in circles, and if it does not march ever onward and upward, how does it move, and where is our place in it? This uncertainty leaves us stuck for the moment in the present, despite our distrust of it. The past no longer seems to us like a benediction, the future no longer appears either predictable or glorious. If time, as we now believe, is a coordinate in space, then its loss signifies in the most literal way a loss of direction. When we do not know what time it is, we cannot know where we are.

Some have taken to calling this the postmodern age. The term places us, semantically, in a new kind of limbo; it cannot be understood literally, since it means "after the present" and can therefore only refer to the future, in which we cannot, as a practical matter, live. *Postmodern* is, moreover, the purest kind of double negative, one that is utterly abstract in that the reference, in fact, is not to the modern, but to modernism, a movement that sought to disavow the past. But there is no intention, in disavowing the disavowal of the past, to embrace it. The term is a denial without any countervailing affirmation. Its meaning is simply, "No!" And it anticipates no sequel. What can possibly, in any literal sense, lie beyond the postmodern? What comes after the future? The only answer we have so far conceived is the mystic one: eternity, the world beyond our world, heaven or hell—or nothing. Postmodernism is the declaration of a future beyond which there is no future. It is, of course, the logical extension of recent intellectual history. In this century God was declared dead, and then history followed. The death of time was only a matter of time.

We may disavow time, but we cannot dispel it. Our own mortality, if nothing else, obligates us to life within its boundaries, and our bodies tie us physically to place. Here is one of the ways in which it is fashionable to deny our earthbound bodies: "Oh, I am not much interested in landscapes," a writer will say, "except as backgrounds.

What interests me is *people.*" As if this constitutes a viable
distinction, as if a person might be understood without
reference to time and place, as if the earth and all its
tens of millions of other species—not to mention the
elemental materials from which life was created—were
merely a trivial detail!

Just as a new myth of earth is emerging—one in
which we see earth as a single, interdependent, self-
regulating organism—so a new view of time has recently
become possible. One might call it relative time, or evolutionary time. It would understand time neither as static
—as in the old myth of cyclicity—nor as mechanical—
as in the more recent myth of progress—but as dynamic:
an unfolding set of creative variations upon a finite set
of basic materials. Such a view would allow us to accept
both change and continuity as aspects of time without
vilifying or deifying either, freeing it from the straitjacket
of our neo-Victorian fundamentalism, which sees the
past as villainy, the present as conspiracy, and the future
as tragedy.

The particular promise of evolutionary time is that
it calls us to place. When we reassert our sense of time,
and our obligation to live within it, we also call ourselves
homeward, since we understand time to be the fourth
dimension of place. But what does it mean to be at
home?

It means primarily that we are called to lives in particular places. There is a way of reading human history,
from the end of the hunting-and-gathering phase onward, as a series—although not necessarily as a progres-
sion—of attempts to find order in abstraction. Wes
Jackson suggests this shorthand reading of the series: the
tribe, the church, the nation-state, the global economy.
Two things strike about this reading: first, each phase

constitutes an escalation in abstraction that denies effective local variation; and second, each is progressively shorter in duration. The idea of ordering our affairs around a global economy has flourished only in this century, and it is already breaking down. The rapidity of its passing, in itself, ought to tell us something.

There is a third pattern to be seen in this reading of history. The more abstract our organizing principles are, the more distant from the disciplines of nature and of local need, the more aggressively extractive and exploitative our lives become: tribal communities lived in North America more or less within the bounds of its ecological carrying capacity; the agrarian economy that supplanted them drew down the accumulated wealth of the land but maintained more or less intact communities; the global economy of the last half century has brought both the accelerated depletion of our natural wealth *and* a radical maldistribution of population with an attendant decline in community vigor. We are increasingly divided among cities too big to be managed, towns too small and isolated to be satisfying, and suburbs that prey upon both: the countryside for wealth and the city for cultural amenities. This is plainly not the result we intended, nor is it a state of affairs sustainable in the long run.

The emerging idea of ecology as an organizing principle opens new standards for judging the suitability of our social arrangements:

- We will judge the strength of society as a whole by the health of its local communities. If gains in one place come at the expense of the viability of another place, we will count the cost too high.
- We will judge the health of local communities on the basis of its most vulnerable members' needs. This

means we will be wary of reasoning from statistical averages. A community in which ten people are starving and ten are obese will not yield, on average, twenty people — or even two — who are well nourished. The deceptions inherent in averages — upon which much conventional economic and social thinking depends — have been exposed by the work of the ecologists. Ecologists have come to understand, for example, how a pothole that holds surface water for only a few spring days a year can be instrumental in sustaining prairie waterfowl populations. Although, on average, it is dry land, such a pothole can properly be described — contrary to both conventional wisdom and common sense — as a wetland. Apparently ephemeral constituents of human communities may also have vital roles to play in their health, invisible though they may be in analyses that depend upon averages and means. Ecological insights give fresh meaning to ancient concerns for justice.

- We will see that some communities are less brittle than others, and we will come to value resiliency in our social and technological designs. Several principles will guide our search for resiliency:
  - Insular communities are more brittle than connected ones.
  - Diversity, as a general rule, promotes resiliency.
  - Dispersed populations are more resilient, as a general rule, than intensively localized ones.
  - The bigger the communities, the fewer the ecosphere can sustain.
  - The farther a community is from its basic resources, the less power it has to manage them.
  - The farther a community strays from its natural condition, the more brittle it becomes.

- The more specialized a community becomes, the less resilient it is.
- Whatever a community does not limit, it cannot ultimately control.

- We will come to understand that we have the adage "Think globally, act locally" backwards. A good abstraction may be made from an adequate number of particulars, but it is exceedingly difficult, if not impossible, to make a good particular from any number of abstractions. We will learn to think locally and to act globally — to act, that is, as if what we do locally matters globally, as indeed it does. This is one of the useful insights to be gained from chaos theory.

- Two common strategies of nature will temper the excessive value our culture has placed on consolidation: redundancy and the use of multiple survival strategies. The principle of redundancy suggests that if the choice is between one huge organization and an array of smaller ones, the most productive and least damaging alternative is likely to be the latter. We know, for example, that in business most new jobs are created by quite small companies, that in farming moderately sized farms are more efficient by most measures than big ones, that in education it is more effective to teach students in groups of twenty than in groups of two hundred, that in wildlife management a network of small ponds is more productive than a single large body of water, and that in community development a neighborhood of moderately sized buildings is likely to be safer and more manageable than one in which people are stacked in towers. But somehow, when we get around to social planning, we forget such models; perhaps the most glaring and persistent falsehood in public-policy circles is the peculiar expectation that consolidation will routinely promote efficiency. This approach to social planning prevents us from asking certain essential questions: Should megacities be saved? Should we direct our policy efforts toward a more reasonable distribution of the population across the landscape?

The principle of multiple survival strategies suggests that good public policy plans from the beginning for a variety of contingencies. A prairie grass survives the periodic stress of severe drought because it is not committed to a single strategy for reproduction. If conditions permit, it will reproduce by seed, yet a single species of grass is still genetically diverse in this respect; the seeds from ten different plants may be programmed to sprout at ten slightly different times, only one or two of which may prove right for the conditions of a particular year. In a year when none of the seeds sprout, however, the plants may still reproduce by means of underground stolens. The same plants can hasten flowering and fruiting in an effort to get ahead of a drought. They can also choose, under the most adverse conditions, to make no effort at all at reproduction, to store such energy as they can collect in their roots, and to wait for more promising circumstances. Because the species is not inflexibly tied to any single strategy for reproduction, the odds exponentially increase that some of its members will persist despite severe stress. Our own economic planning, in particular, might take this model to heart.

All of these suggestions have one thing in common: they follow from thinking about human communities in ecological terms, from imagining that were we to see ourselves as "natural," as belonging to nature, and were we to live within the patterns and constraints of nature, we might make for ourselves a more stable and secure future. There is something humbling about this, of course. We have already several times revised our estimate of our place in the universe. Once we thought that earth was all there was to the universe. Then we discovered the solar system, but thought that we were at the center of it. When that idea failed, we settled for an image of human beings as at the domineering center of life on earth. Now that idea has failed, too, and we see that we must be resigned to understanding ourselves as one species among many living a mysterious existence in the outer reaches of a minor galaxy in an infinite universe.

But there is something exalted about this new self-image, too. With every downward revision in our estimate of ourselves, we have more clearly seen ourselves to be participants in a universe infinitely complex and intertwined. What we have sacrificed in pretension, we have more than gained in intimacy with a place ever more astonishingly grand. It is an ancient principle of spirituality that whoever would be exalted must first be humbled. We feel the truth of that insight now more keenly than ever as we prepare to step from the limbo of eternity into the vast wonder of time.

**4**

# Dreaming in West Bend, Iowa

W EST BEND is a small farming
community in northern Iowa
only a couple of hours from my
house. One does not come across
such a place by happenstance. It
is not on the way to anywhere.
Either you intend to go there or, like a thousand other
little towns in rural America, it will be as lost to you
as some minor star in the Milky Way. Most strangers
who arrive there have come to see the Grotto of the
Redemption, advertised as the largest construction of
its kind in the world.

Even for prairieland, the countryside around West Bend is strikingly featureless. The land is so flat that, as you pull off the nearest major highway nine miles away, you can already see the town's grain elevators above its mostly two-story skyline. The earth in such landscapes seems thin and fragile, nothing more than a sliver of crust floating in the vast sky, forever in danger of being swamped and sunk by the blue universe. The soil itself is black and thick, some of the richest farmland in the world, as any native will tell you. But its richness is not apparent to those who do not till it: how could something so plain and horizontal, so unsparkling, so unadorned, be rich in any way worth mentioning?

West Bend itself belies the wealth of its soils; it is as plain and unassuming as the countryside surrounding it. The wealth of the land has not, in general, translated into riches for its people, and even if it had, one of the rural values still somewhat surviving in places like West Bend is the unseemliness of making a show of wealth.

It is the sort of place in which a half-block-square, four-story-high construction studded with one and a half million dollars worth of precious and semiprecious gemstones is bound to look as imposing as a mountain. Such is the Grotto of the Redemption, an edifice created, mainly, by one man, living on a priest's salary and laboring for almost a half century, the first forty years of which without so much as the aid of a power tool.

God knows what the raw young village must have looked like to German-born Paul M. Dobberstein when he arrived there in 1897 to take charge of Saints Peter and Paul's Catholic Church, a new church in a newly organized diocese. He was a brand-new priest, beginning his work in a nation to which he had immigrated only five years earlier. It must have seemed to him that he had gone literally to the ends of the earth to preach the Gospel.

There he remained until his death at 7:25 P.M. on July 24, 1954. A measure of the regard for his work is that the precise minute of his passing is known, and the townspeople still take it as a sign of his favor with God that he was permitted to live until the eventide of his last sunny day on mortal earth. And it is a measure of the times in which he labored that he was tolerated by the same congregation—and that he tolerated it—for fifty-seven years. We are no longer used to such steadfastness of resolve.

From the moment Father Dobberstein arrived in West Bend, people say, he had in mind a plan for the Grotto of the Redemption. The story, which has the flavor of hagiography, is that as a seminarian Dobberstein was stricken with pneumonia and prayed to the Virgin Mary for his life, promising to build her a shrine if he were saved.

I do not believe the promise part of the story. Father Dobberstein might well have built a shrine in gratitude for his life. Certainly he had a keen sense of his mortality. The brief account of his life includes references to three other narrow escapes: a 1928 car crash, while hunting for stones near Dubuque, Iowa, that disabled him for six months; a scaffolding collapse from which he escaped with only a sprained ankle; and, again searching for stones, in South Dakota, a dynamite explosion on the road just minutes ahead of him. These stories would not be told now if Father Dobberstein himself had not made something of them. But I cannot believe, looking at his handiwork, that he was the sort of man who would think that the Virgin Mary bargains lives for monuments.

Whatever the reason, he began to collect materials for the monument shortly after he arrived in West Bend. By 1901 he had arranged to purchase a suitable parcel of land at the west edge of town. His first task was to excavate a pond and to plant a ring of birches around it. The birches have since died, but other trees have replaced them and the pond remains. A couple of white swans swim in it, giving the place an Old Country look, as, perhaps, he intended. In 1912, a decade before the completion even of a permanent place of worship, he had started to build the Grotto of the Trinity, the first of the seven he was destined to complete at West Bend. (He was also commissioned to build eight lesser grottoes and monuments in small Midwest cities ranging from LaCrosse, Wisconsin, to Parkston, South Dakota.)

Dobberstein meant to make something that would last. "Spoken words are ephemeral: written words remain, but their durability depends upon the material upon which they are written: but if carved in bronze or sculptured in stone they are well nigh imperishable," he wrote. "This imperishableness is the outstanding feature of the Grotto." The sermon in stone that he created is undergirded with steel; every one of the hundreds of thousands of rocks and gems that ornament it was hand chipped to fit snugly into the rich mixture of Portland cement that he used as mortar; and the cement itself he tended like a newborn baby, watering each batch every four hours, night and day, for a week to be sure that it would cure properly. Parts of the grotto have now withstood three-quarters of a century of violent prairie weather and the footsteps and prying fingers of millions of visitors, and yet one is hard pressed to find a crack or sign of wear anywhere in it.

Dobberstein worked without blueprints or drawings.

He translated directly from imagination into stone. But of course he was working from a text. The Grotto of the Trinity, for example, is constructed in three arched half circles to represent the three persons of God. Into one of these is set a stained-glass window showing the angel Gabriel announcing to Mary that she is the chosen mother of Christ, and above it is a quarter moon, the symbol of the Immaculate Mary. Set into the second half circle is a statue (in fine white Carrara marble from Italy) of Mary cradling the baby Jesus in her arms, above it is the Star of Bethlehem with its comet's tail, and above the star, the word *Ave,* in Venetian glass covered with gold leaf, is written upside down to symbolize that our blessings come from heaven and not from earth. Set in the third half circle is a cross, and above it is a sun to symbolize the light of Christ and Christ as the Sun of Justice. And above all these Father Dobberstein made a dome, narrow at the opening and expansive on the interior, into which he set many bejeweled stars—a vision of heaven.

The symbolism laid in mosaic into the solid walls of this little grotto does not by any means end there. Under Mary's feet lies a serpent, a symbol of victory over temptation. Two streams of water flow down the walls and into a basin, symbolizing the two persons of Christ. The symbols of the Passion are there: the hammer, the nails, the sponge with which Christ was offered a drink of vinegar and gall, the spear with which his heart was pierced, the crown of thorns with which he was mocked. I suppose even that there are meanings in those stones that Father Dobberstein carried to the grave.

After this first grotto, Father Dobberstein labored for another forty years to tell the whole story of his faith in stone. He was a busy man, serving often as the sole priest in his parish, baptizing almost a thousand babies,

instructing children in the school for which the corner-
stone was laid in 1899 (he was very thorough, his
assistant in later years remembered), and supervising
the construction of a handsome new church in 1922
and of a restaurant to accommodate the crowds that by
the late 1920s had begun to flock to West Bend to pay
homage at his shrine. In those days, too, he somehow
found the time to put aside his hammer and to take pil-
grims on personal tours. And still he felt compelled to
build: turreted walls around the church grounds and a
stone pool at its entrance; in the sanctuary a Christmas
Chapel of materials too precious to be outside (among
them a 2,000-pound amethyst, a string of pearls, and a
collection of polished agates); shrines in other cities;
and six more grottos depicting the Garden of Eden, the
Ten Commandments, the Twelve Stations of the Cross,
and the crucifixion, burial, and resurrection of Jesus.

He had the time through all of this to be both
playful and funny. Playful: In the Grotto of the Ten
Commandments a stalactite, taken from Jewel Cave in
South Dakota's Black Hills, hangs from the ceiling.
When Dobberstein installed it, he included in the ceiling
above it a deposit of calcium and a conduit for rainwater
so that the stalactite would continue to grow just as it had
in its natural setting. The scheme works. The formation
has been growing at the rate of an eighth of an inch
every thirty years. Funny: On the way to Mount Calvary,
there is a staircase leading nowhere. It is paved with
barite "roses," wind-sculpted bits of rock that resemble
the flower. He made the staircase, Father Dobbersetin
said, to remind people that the way to heaven is not
through a bed of roses.

He planned one more grotto, the Grotto of the
Ascension, which he hoped would be the most glorious of

all, but he met his own ascension before he could begin it.

The additions since have not been improvements: two inferior grottos; a system of loudspeakers over which chimes continuously play, giving the place the ambiance of a funeral parlor; and a videotaped "geology" lecture in which a good deal of time is spent hustling souvenirs and donations "in case you might be interested."

I wish the place had been left as it was. It is Father Dobberstein's work, the work of his life, and it is not likely now to be improved. Adding to it, even skillfully, is like trying to amend a life already lived.

I visited Father Dobberstein's grottos like any tourist, and then I went back one late-summer evening, hoping that I might glimpse what he himself had seen there. It was one of the first fall-like nights after the awful heat of a droughty year, and the air felt blessedly cool. The fields of corn and soybeans were ripening. Their browns looked golden in the elongated rays of the reddening sun. Flocks of blackbirds rose and settled among the tall rows of corn like dark waves.

It was after supper in the little town. In some windows the lights were just beginning to glimmer. Main Street was deserted. Long minutes slipped by when nothing moved along the avenues, and then a car would pass, the crunching of its tires sounding as plaintive as a dog barking in the night.

There were half a dozen visitors at the Grotto when I arrived. They shuffled silently along while the chimes sounded. I could hear the words of the hymn in my mind:

*Just as I am without one plea,*
*But that thy blood was shed for me*
*And that thou biddest me come to Thee.*
*Oh, Lamb of God, I come, I come.*

The visitors left. A priest came out of the rectory, passed down a sidewalk, and disappeared behind a pair of American elms somehow unravaged by disease, tall and thick, their crowns cascading like fireworks. I wondered if Father Dobberstein had planted them and the stately maples in the churchyard. They looked the right age.

The crickets in the grass played a quivering ostinato on the C above middle C. On the pond a teal quacked. A brood of Canada geese grazed along the shore, quiet for once.

In the lighted window of the restaurant, I could see a young woman cleaning up. Liver and onions was the special of the evening, a sign said, but there were no takers. When I approached the Grotto of the Empty Tomb I flushed a sparrow and it made me start.

*Oh, Lamb of God, I come, I come.*

It was so peaceful there, so quiet and undisturbed, that it seemed to me like the serenity of the wilderness. I wandered as in a wild place, uncertain what to expect, alert, alive in a way that one seldom is under the daily assault of the familiar. The feel of the place brought back to me evenings when I wandered as a boy and marveled at everything, at the wideness of the sky, at the leaves of corn whispering in the breeze, at the ring of creamy light along the horizon after the sun had set and the colors of day had faded, at the emerging stars. It was then, as almost never since, that everything seemed possible.

I thought that it must have been on such evenings that Father Dobberstein's plans for a great grotto at West Bend sprouted and took root. He would not have thought the idea outrageous on such a night, even though there is scarcely a stone in all the surrounding countryside. They are so rare that a nearby town was

named after one: Lone Rock. But stones could be found,
mountains could be raised up, the faithful would follow.
When you reach a certain stage of loneliness or isolation
you begin to dream out loud.

I climbed to the top of Calvary and from there, forty
feet up, I could see what I have seen from mountaintops:
the great expanse of earth curving away toward unreach-
able horizons. The Plains Indians said that everywhere
was the center of the world, and so it is.

We are always in danger of conceding that truth,
those of us who live in out-of-the-way places. We are forever tempted to believe that the real world is somewhere
else, or, worse, that the world has no other center but
ours. How often has it been said that ours are the sleepy
places, and how often have we accepted the label? How
often have we congratulated ourselves as the keepers
of the simple virtues? The truth is that we are all at the
center of something, and no place automatically confers
either virtue or simplicity. Human nature is human nature; it does not vary from census to census. We all stand
in need of redemption.

To believe otherwise is to give up dreaming.

Father Dobberstein might have lived out his life as a
dutiful priest in a sleepy Iowa town a long way from anywhere. He might have gone around saying, "In case you
might be interested." But I can't imagine such words
falling from his lips. He had a dream of a great grotto,
and since he was in West Bend, he dreamed that it might
be there. Then he built it. Preposterous as it was, he built
it. And so he made a monument to the redemptive and
imperishable power of our dreams.

## Visions

WHEN I WAS A SMALL BOY, my twin sister and I shared a bed in the single bedroom of our house. Our parents slept in the big bed at the far end of the room, and we slept in the smaller one near the door. The long, narrow, low-ceilinged dimensions of the room made its windows, which were of standard size, seem extravagantly large. They faced east and south, catching, on clear nights, the moonlight, which had a soft blue radiance and in which bits of dust swirled like the crystals of snow in the glass globe that my grandmother kept on

her dining-room bureau. In the wintertime, the flame of
the oil-burning stove in the next room flickered through
the isinglass, giving off an intermittent orange-and-yellow
glow that danced on the door frame. Occasionally a car
would pass on the gravel road not twenty feet beyond the
windows, suddenly filling the room with blinding light
and as suddenly plunging it again into darkness.

I took a long time in falling asleep as a small child.
That bedroom was too vibrant with various emanations
of light to encourage easy sleep. As I lay watching the
shadows ebb and flow, trying to catch the gossamer particles of things floating in the moonbeams, and listening
to the stirrings in the next bed, to the scampering of
mice in the hollow walls, to the movement of the air beyond the windows, and to the faint creakings and groan-
ings of the old house, the strange world of the night, of
which I was vaguely fearful, would stir to life and I, however sleepy I had been at bedtime, would waken with it.

If I were to lie awake long enough, I would see a
ghost. The form was that of a very tall man with long
arms and lanky legs, and it wore a dark Stetson and cowboy boots with sharp toes and spurs on the heels that
glinted in what little light there was. Despite its boots
and the fact that the floor was covered in linoleum, the
ghost moved soundlessly and with the exaggerated, fly-
ing motions of a dancer. It looked like one of those blue
dancers in the jazz collages by Matisse, although the
apparition was not blue but a gray-brown with the shade
and texture of felt, like a grainy photograph printed
in sepia.

I can give you a precise picture of this ghost because
I saw it several dozen times over the period of a year and
a half and because my sister, who was there beside me,
saw exactly the same thing. We had not made the image

up. Neither of us had ever seen a cowboy, or a dancer for
that matter, much less a cutout of one by Matisse. We did
not have a television set, we were not allowed to go to the
movies, and the only books in our house that we might
have looked at were a collection of Mother Goose
rhymes and a volume of Bible stories for children, neither of which showed a picture of a cowboy.

True, we played Cowboys and Indians, as white kids
did in rural Minnesota in the early 1950s—this ghost
appeared to us beginning in the spring of 1952—but
nobody in our set ever wanted to be a cowboy, and so we
were all Indians and the cowboys were the imaginary
enemy, just over the hill or just beyond the shadows of
the grove, against whom we fought, always victoriously.
Cowboys could have looked like anything, so far as we
knew.

The ghost was so tall that it had to duck to pass
through the doorway into the bedroom. The figure
darted to and fro, like the branch of a tree in the wind,
just at the foot of our bed, as if it were looking for something to steal—perhaps my sister and me as we cowered
under our covers. When we cried out in unison, it fled,
sometimes back through the doorway, sometimes out the
east window at the foot of our bed. Both my sister and I
saw it leave, and our opinions on which way it had gone
always agreed.

Sometimes, if we had drifted off to sleep, the ghost
would pull at our toes, perhaps trying to get hold of us to
carry us off, and we would awaken to see it fleeing, either
out the same window or through the same doorway. It
came as often as two or three times a week and as seldom
as two or three times a month, more frequently in the
summertime than in the winter, although we suspected
that the ghost visited in the winter too, when the room

was too dark for us to perceive it. We sometimes felt the sensation of an unseen presence, perhaps in the irregular currents of the air.

Our father soon learned that he could not poohpooh the veracity of what we had seen and urge us to go back to sleep. We could not sleep again until he demonstrated that the ghost was gone. So he would get up, light a lamp, pull back all the bedcovers and show us that nothing was there, invite us to peer under the bed with him, take us on a tour of the other two rooms in the house until we had seen for ourselves that the ghost had gone away. Then, for extra measure, he would bolt the door to the exterior of the house so that the ghost, if it were still lurking about outdoors, could not get back in again. When this ritual had been completed, we were quite content, after the first several episodes, to go back to sleep, since we knew from experience that the ghost never came twice in the same night.

The rural world of forty years ago predated the demythologizing of everything. Ghosts, apparitions, and ethereal messages of many kinds were still given credence in that world. The barkless hulk of an old cottonwood tree in the corner of the grove on our place gleamed in an unearthly way in the moonlight. We children knew that it was haunted by a ghost—perhaps the ghost we saw in the bedroom—one proof of its presence for us being the fact that a great horned owl with enormous yellow eyes liked to perch in it. The sort of wisdom that owls possess, of course, is of the spirit world.

In the world of my youth, you planted potatoes on the night of the first full moon after Easter, if your nose itched you knew that somebody was talking about you, and when you killed a snake, you had to hang it by its tail in a place where the first rays of sunrise would shine into its eyes, or it would spring back to life again. Snakes had lives in those days that persisted beyond the body.

I grew to manhood and put away childish things, or so I would have said. One night during our time in Washington, D. C., my wife and I went out to a dinner party. I am the sort of person who hates the thought of a party and has to be harangued and cajoled into attending one but, when I finally get there, have to be asked by the host in the early hours of the morning to please leave and come back another day.

The party we attended that night was a typical Washington affair—a good deal of jockeying for position of the "And who are you with?" sort, a surfeit of booze, and no sign for hours on end of anything resembling dinner. We had just been launched into the buzz of chatter fueled by spirits and incipient malnourishment —the dinner to which we had been invited was still a good hour away—when suddenly I felt the overwhelming urge to leave that house as quickly as possible and to get home. My wife, when I confided in her, looked at me with alarm and disbelief, but she saw that I was serious, even desperate, and acquiesced. We called a cab, apologized to our host, and hurried home.

As we entered the front door, the telephone was ringing. It was my mother on the line with the news that my father had just died. He had died, in fact, at the very moment when I had succumbed to some unknown anxiety at the party.

I sat for a long time that night in the dimly lit living room of our house, listening to the Bach B Minor Mass and struggling to have any coherent thought. Then I saw in the corner of the room, quite distinctly, the ghost of a man with long arms and lanky legs, wearing a Stetson

and cowboy boots with spurs. He wavered there for a
minute, swaying like a dancer, and then vanished
through the window. In the stillness of his departure, I
found the strength, at last, to weep.

Many years later, I traversed the Bob Marshall Wilderness
in northwestern Montana with a friend. The Bob
Marshall is one of the last refuges of the grizzly bear, a
fact we had been edgily aware of the whole trip. One
night we camped in a peaceful grove of pines nestled
against the Chinese Wall, a spectacular, thousand-foot-
high, thirteen-mile-long escarpment at the heart of the
wilderness. At dusk a strong wind arose, howling over the
Divide and whistling in the tops of the trees. The walls of
our tent, when we retired for the night, fluttered and
flapped. It would have blown away had we not weighed it
down. Although it was the middle of the summer, the
high-pitched whine of the wind carried the sound of winter and of death — bleak, desolate, mournful. Then the
wind grew calmer, murmuring in the trees like water
tumbling over rocks. We might have been, from the
sound of it, camped beside the gentle falls of a river.

I awoke in the night, chilled, perhaps by the sugges-
tive voice of the wind, for the air itself was mild. I had
the strong sense that we were in the presence of another
creature. John felt it and awoke, too. I reached for my
glasses and rose on my elbows, but it was utterly dark,
impossible to make out anything. We listened intently,
but nothing could be heard above the wind. For a long
time I listened. Then the sensation passed. We seemed
alone again. I fell asleep. In the morning, the air was
tranquil and the sun sparkled on a heavy dew. We
looked for tracks in the vicinity of our tent, but it was a
grassy place and tracks would not easily have been seen

even had they been there. Whether we had been awakened by imagination, or prescience, or premonition we
would never know.

The next night at dusk, as we set up a tent along a fork of
the Sun River, the strong feeling of foreboding returned.
I was securing the last tent pole in its grommet when
John, who had turned toward the river, touched my
shoulder and said quietly, "They're here, Paul."
     By the time I could set the tent down and turn
around, a sow grizzly bear had reached the place where
our packs were hanging. She was enormous and blonde.
The silver tips of her venerable hair glistened in the long
angle of the sunlight filtering through the trees. She did
not make a sound as she moved with athletic grace toward her purpose, her massive shoulders as fluid as
water. She was like a waterfall on legs. The hump of her
back was so prominent and her size so great, that in another setting I might temporarily have mistaken her for a
bison cow. She did not waste a motion or hesitate for a
microsecond. She was completely, assuredly in charge.
Behind her trailed two darker cubs, themselves the size
of black bears. We realized that she had been there all
along, lurking in the willows while we ate and bathed
and sallied at the edge of the river, biding her time,
watching us, awaiting her opportunity.
     Adrenaline flooded into my bloodstream. I was high
on it before I knew it. When I opened my mouth to
speak, I had difficulty catching my breath and the words
quavered. "She is very beautiful, isn't she?" I said softly.
She was, in the old and religious sense, awesome, mes-
merizing in her grace and power, perfectly formed in
every way.
     We moved a few feet into the screen of some tall

shrubs, a gesture that reassured us while doing nothing
to secure our safety. Grizzly bears have notoriously bad
eyes but keen ears and incomparable noses. The old
adage is that if a pine needle falls in the forest, the eagle
sees it, the deer hears it, and the bear smells it. We had
been hiking for nine days without benefit of thorough
baths. We stank even to ourselves. She could certainly, in
the right wind, have smelled us a mile away (an odor
Andy Russell, who knows grizzlies as intimately as anybody, describes as offensive, from a bear's point of view,
to the point of nausea), and we were scarcely a hundred
feet from her, a distance she could have covered before
the charge had registered in our brains. Even so, we continued to whisper to each other as we watched. We were,
suddenly, delirious.

The bear used the same foothold I had used to get
up one of the anchor trees, stretched her massive right
front paw — its long claws glinting — ten feet up, seized
the rope, and thwacked it up and down until John's pack
slid toward her. Then she clamped one of its straps in
her teeth, pulled it toward her, and snapped the aluminum frame in half in her powerful forearms, as if it
were a twig. She let the pieces fall to the ground,
grabbed the slackened rope between her teeth, and cut
it. My pack crashed down. We laughed.

"Well, there's the end of our hike," John said
cheerfully.

"I suppose it's a little like watching your house burn,"
I said. That seemed hilarious to us, too.

I was thinking of the spectacle of fire. There was the
hypnotic energy of fire in the bear's movements: the rig-
orous efficiency with which she undid our best precau-
tions against her, the intelligence so belying our arrogant
presumptions against animal thought. We were captive

not only to her power but to her wit, which had proved
superior to ours.

While the darker cubs, looking too big for it, gam-
boled in the shadows, the adult grizzly set methodically
about her work. She ripped apart the packs and searched
the scattered contents, item by item, for edibles. We had
intended to go out the next day to resupply; the pickings
were slim, but she overlooked nothing. I knew how resourceful grizzlies can be in their diets, in ways that
sometimes seem incongruous, given their size—of their
fondness for ants, for ladybugs, and for the dainty strawberries that grow so profusely on the Montana front
range.

She had an indiscriminate palate and a forgiving
stomach. She snapped up freeze-dried foods in their foil-
lined packages, gorp, candies, tea bags and pipe tobacco,
toothpaste. She helped herself to bottles of sunscreen, vi-
tamins, aspirins, antihistamine and Kaopectate tablets,
paper and plastic, shards of cloth. She sampled bottles of
insect repellent and canisters of white gas. She punc-
tured water bottles, which popped like balloons. She
latched her massive jaws around the nest of cooking pots
and chomped down, puncturing them with what looked,
when we inspected them later, like rifle bullet holes.
Perhaps she had a bad tooth; at any rate, after the sound
of lacerating metal came a particularly robust roar, one
of half a dozen she sent echoing through the sparkling
air of the narrow valley.

Doug Peacock, another man intimately familiar with
grizzlies, describes that roar as capable of "chilling your
piss." Perhaps it is, in other circumstances. Peacock, after
all, claims to have survived more than forty bear charges.
This was only the third time I had seen one in the wild.
But those roars—directed at what, we could not tell—

sounded to me magnificent, not chilling, even though a shiver ran down my spine. The bear's voice was as enormous and commanding as its physique—grander, less guttural, and more eloquent than the roars of the one lion I have heard.

"I felt," John wrote me later, "like I was approaching the throne of the 'most high.' While the grizzly was dismantling our property, and clearly ignoring us, I was thinking about what I've always been taught—everything we have in life, including life itself, is a gift. I understand that intellectually, but watching and listening to her and knowing she could wipe us out any time she wanted to, I understood emotionally about gifts."

The bear used her long, razor-sharp claws as adroitly as fingers. There was a single hard candy in the right pocket of my denim hiking shorts. She extracted and ate it, leaving only a slight tear in the shorts. She cut a quarter moon in a leather binoculars case without scratching the binoculars themselves. She shredded the stuff sack holding my sleeping bag but left the bag itself uncut. She ripped a sack holding a down vest, leaving the vest intact.

We watched her at close range for some time, spellbound and joyful. In our helplessness we had lost our fear. It felt liberating to be, for once, in charge of absolutely nothing.

Then it dawned on us that we might be safer at a greater distance. We backed cautiously away from the bear. She did not so much as glance in our direction. If she was aware of us, she ignored us with grand disdain. I have often felt such disregard in the presence of wild animals. Although I have sometimes been dismayed, I have come to cherish that lack of interest as a useful corrective, a reminder that only in our own inflated imaginations do human beings star in the center ring of creation.

By stages, we made our way out of the forest and up a steep grassy ridge. About halfway up we found a comfortable place to sit, a couple of hundred yards from the bear. We could still, indistinctly in the fading light, make out her movements. Mainly we heard her, a steady staccato of rips, shreds, and pops, accentuated now and then by a roar, perhaps of pain or frustration, or as a warning against interference, or simply for the hell of it.

We counted our blessings. How fortunate that the bear had arrived while it was still light; that she had not surprised us in our tent; that she had permitted us to get out of the way before moving in; that we were so close to the edge of the wilderness, hours rather than days from food and shelter; that we had been granted this rare, close encounter with one of the earth's legendary creatures. We congratulated each other on our luck.

"Let's face it," John said, "this is the moment you've been searching for." I had in fact once said, recklessly, that I would welcome any encounter with a grizzly bear, even one that did me injury, so long as I might be permitted to survive. In the motel room in Great Falls, the night before we had gone up to Marias Pass to begin our walk, we had read of an early morning attack on a hiker in Yellowstone National Park. The woman, alone, had come around a bend in the trail, surprising a mother grizzly with cubs at close range. She had been grievously, but not fatally, wounded. From her hospital bed, silenced by a tracheotomy, she had penned a plea for the bear. It had only been doing its maternal duty, she said; she held no ill will toward it.

I had often noticed that reaction in stories I had read about encounters with bears. It cheered me. Such willingness to submit to the authority of a prior claim by another species, even in the advent of harm, is rare in our culture, almost as rare as the grizzlies themselves. These encounters sometimes show us what it still means to live with humility in the world. The grizzly bear is almost uniquely capable of commanding such respect; for that reason alone its survival among us is vital. The point is not, as it is so often put, that we fear it, and that it is good for us to know fear—although that is also true—but that the grizzly demands of us some fealty to its own nature.

There was, at last, a long silence. We began to think that the bear had left. Then there was the sound again of rending fabric. Later, we would see that she had left the campground and sought out our tent, which we had erected but not staked, shredding its sides and flattening it, mangling its aluminum poles. This one act seemed gratuitous. It peeved me. The tent was nine days old, empty, and had never been near food or been slept in in clothing that had come into contact with food.

After that, we followed her progress eastward through the forest toward Benchmark, audible in the series of cracks of sticks and small timber, like firecrackers exploding. The bursts grew fainter and finally faded away altogether. We sat for some minutes after they had dissipated, listening breathlessly to be sure that she was gone. When we were certain of it, we exhaled pent-up air and rose to our feet. We were surprised to notice that it was already night, that the air was chilly, and that the nearly full moon had come up over the ridge. Never had a night seemed so tranquil.

We went down in the moonlight as far as the tent, reflecting the blue glow like a pool of water, and looked for our sleeping bags. Improbably, they had survived. The stillness of the forest was eerie, so encased, so riddled with menacing shadows. Everything seemed alive in

the place now, nothing necessarily stationary or benign:
the trees, the thin layer of soil, the rocks, the blue beams
of moonlight glimmering up out of the leaves. We made
quickly for the freedom of the grassy ridge. Near its
peak, below a stand of limber pines, we found a place
where we could lie under the wide, open sky. The hillside
embraced us with a welcoming grace. We wriggled into
our sleeping bags, zipped them up, and prepared to receive whatever the night might bring.

We had been sleeping in forests beside clammering
streams or in the high country where the wind always
blows at night. So I found this night's sounds a revela-
tion. A bat squeaked by. Somewhere a nighthawk
collected a late harvest of insects, its wings buzzing,
a sound familiar on the deserted evening streets of every
prairie village. Upriver an owl called, and downriver
another answered it.

Overhead a star plummeted in a blinding flash, the
brightest either of us had ever seen. Satellites ambled this
way and that. The moon hung over a sensuous line of barren hills, and the big dipper tilted toward the river, as if to
resupply it. I thought of boyhood nights wandering the
countryside of Rosewood Township, listening to the night
breeze in the corn and to the distant barking of dogs and
dumbstruck by the shimmering, vaulting vastness of
space. I felt small and young again, insignificant and secure in my insignificance, kept and attended, all of life's
mystery still stretching out ahead of me, undiscovered.

Suddenly there was a loud, deep twang, like the
sound of a bass fiddle string being plucked. We started.

John sat up in his sleeping bag. "What was that?"
he asked.

"A wood frog," I said, gathering my wits. "A lovelorn
wood frog."

Just when we had forgotten it, the frog called again in its oddly mechanical and impossibly loud way, the sorriest love song in all of nature. One more twang, and it fell silent.

"Not very persistent, either, poor thing," I said.

We were determined to keep a wakeful vigil until the dawn came, out of some sense of circumspection, I suppose. Something about the encounter with the bear—the animal itself, or the violence of the meeting, or the sense of having been spared—required it of us. We had entertained briefly the prospect of early death and had been granted stays of execution. Our lives seemed now acutely fresh and full of promise. It was not a moment one ought to shrug away. So I was chagrined to notice, when I opened the eyes I had been resting only for a moment, that the moon had gone down. Above me arched the Milky Way, so dense with stars that they looked, to my dim eyes, continuous, unfathomable, a great radiance at the heart of the universe. For the second time that night I felt tiny and secure, untouched by any prospect except to savor the one before me.

And then the hour before dawn arrived, crisp and clear, the breathless hour when even the animals seem to pause and ponder, the universal hour of reverie. A golden halo of light bathed the grassy ridge tops, but the forest and the river below were still cast in heavy shadow. Our sleeping bags were covered with frost, and inside them we were lightly dressed. We awaited the benediction of the sun.

It was a long time in coming, as something anticipated always is. When it appeared, we wriggled out of our bags, shook the frost from them, put on our boots and our hats, and went down the ridge toward the river. The slope was long and astonishingly steep, so steep that we had difficulty in keeping our footing as we eased down it on all fours. We did not have, that morning, adrenaline-powered feet with which to clamber. They felt leaden and clumsy again, as one's feet do in the first and last hours of the day. We had known, briefly, fleetness, and now we were back to putting one foot forward at a time.

We felt, too, a kind of shyness as we crossed the trail and entered the grove where we had begun what seemed an eternity ago to make a camp. I suppose it was not shyness but a sense of trespass, of having presumed to claim a place that was not, after all, ours.

We found the tatters of our things scattered for fifty feet in every direction. It was peaceful and sunny there, like the morning after a storm. We poked through the rubble, looking for what we might salvage: our rain jackets, the binoculars, our spoons and cups, our jackknives, a few feet of rope. What we could not salvage and had no means to carry, we collected, stuffed into the remnants of our packs, and set along the trail to be hauled out later. It took us the better part of an hour to clean up the mess. When we had finished, we gathered the few items that were still useful, wrapped them in the rain covers for our packs, tied them into bundles with the pieces of rope, and slung them over our walking sticks.

We headed down the trail like a pair of hoboes. In a mile, we joined the tracks of the bears. By and by, we met an outfitter, long and lanky and looking dashing in his silver spurs and broad-rimmed Stetson, who was leading twenty-one heavily laden mules upriver in advance of a party of vacationers. He surveyed us with unconcealed contempt. Just as he passed, he leaned toward us. "Making a lot of progress that way, boys?" he drawled.

We let the remark pass. We were filled that morning with the meekness of angels.

I have been thinking since then about the paradox that although we humans are preeminently creatures of sight — so much so that the verb "to see" is synonymous in our language with the verb "to understand." Still, we are forever catching sight of things that could not possibly exist or finding that what we thought we saw was actually something else altogether. A maurauding bear ought to be an apparition of terror, but what I saw, in the moment of its fulfillment, was a vision of beauty. Perhaps, as Antoine de Saint Exupéry once wrote, "What is essential is invisible to the eye." In any case, there is a vast difference between sight and vision: sight is something we can know about, improve, repair, but vision is another matter entirely.

A vision, I have been thinking, is probably, in this respect, a lot like a grizzly bear that appears at her own will or like a ghost that shows up at odd hours and vanishes when you go looking for it.

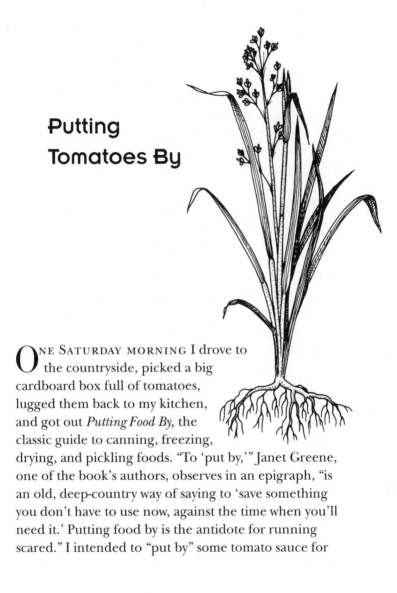

## Putting
## Tomatoes By

ONE SATURDAY MORNING I drove to
the countryside, picked a big
cardboard box full of tomatoes,
lugged them back to my kitchen,
and got out *Putting Food By,* the
classic guide to canning, freezing,
drying, and pickling foods. "To 'put by,'" Janet Greene,
one of the book's authors, observes in an epigraph, "is
an old, deep-country way of saying to 'save something
you don't have to use now, against the time when you'll
need it.' Putting food by is the antidote for running
scared." I intended to "put by" some tomato sauce for

the winter, something I had not done for years.

There was a trick to preserving the color and fresh taste of canned tomatoes, but I did not remember it. The trick, *Putting Food By* reminded me, is to add ascorbic acid, Vitamin C, which neutralizes the trace minerals in the fruits. Ascorbic acid was sold in grocery stores in crystalline form when people regularly put by their own produce. It is no longer available, at least at my grocery, except in tablet form as a dietary supplement. In this there was probably a metaphor for the American food system, something about food as medicine rather than as sustenance, but I did not work it out. I was intent upon tomato sauce, not philosophy.

I needed a footstool to reach the blue enameled canning kettle that had languished in the cobwebby recesses of the top pantry shelf for years. Why are such pots always blue? Why not red or green or yellow, or simply gray, like the big enameled pots in which egg coffee was once boiled on such state occasions as funerals, school picnics, and family reunions? Perhaps there was some subliminal suggestion of purity in the color, of cloudless skies, of clear waters, of the blueing agent used to whiten clothes washed in hard water with harsh, lye-based soaps.

By the time I did my apprenticeship in home canning in the 1950s, under my mother's watchful eye, the idea had taken hold that it was a perilous undertaking better left to factories, which had superior defenses against such toxins as salmonella and botulism, food-borne illnesses that used to be generically known as ptomaine poisoning. Ptomaine poisoning had entered my vocabulary before I encountered my first Dick and Jane reader, so much was it on our minds in our subsistence household.

By the 1970s, when it seemed as if a new wave of backyard gardeners might again play some role in the national food system, home-extension economists were producing papers with such titles as "The True Cost of Home Food Preservation," demonstrating conclusively that it was cheaper to buy food at the grocery store than to preserve your own. One must consider, the home economists advised, the cost of jars, lids, and kettles, of gas or electricity, of labor in the garden and kitchen; it was an extravagance, really, to try to produce food for one's family.

In our own household, dispassionate and impeccable as the calculations were, such economic analysis did not apply. The investment in equipment for home food production had long since been made and amortized. Mason jars and canning kettles were eminently recyclable; in the early years, the energy came from the woodlot, not from an electrical or gas line; and if we were cash poor, we were rich in time. My mother might have gone to work at some low-paying industrial or clerical job—as a teenager she did work in a canning factory—and in that way we might have afforded the supposedly cheaper foods available at the grocery. But would this have resulted in more time, less labor, or better food? I doubt it. And if the time one takes to produce one's own food is an expense—as it surely is—then why shouldn't one count the comparable investment of time involved in earning the money to buy it? Whether the exchange is for cash or for labor, the time remains unrecompensed. The value expressed in the home-extension kind of analysis is not economic but cultural: wage-earning labor, it assumes, is productive; sustenance-earning labor is not.

Such analysis depends upon a kind of sentimentality. The sort of work my mother did, because it did not generate cash, contributing by default, one could say, to our family's penury, is conventionally described as back breaking, tedious, and soul destroying. This presumes that wage labor is happier, easier, morally superior work (for what is "soul-destroying" work if it is not morally degrading?). We are ever, and properly so, on guard against views of the past that gloss over grim realities. Is it not the same kind of error, which manifests itself in the idea of progress, to romanticize the present?

I am, I suppose, alert to this question because I have pursued my own work, as my mother did hers, without prospect of monetary reward. For the past decade I have devoted myself to writing books. As books go, they have fared reasonably well; they have, at least, stayed in print. Still, I could have quadrupled my earnings had I spent my time slinging hamburgers in a fast-food outlet. I can imagine a paper by an economist on "The True Cost of Writing Books." I suppose it would point out that while I have earned something from my books, if I consider the value of my time, the expenses of paper and postage, of my desk and chair, of my computer and printer and the electricity to run them, and of research, I have in fact operated at a rather large deficit. It would surely, from an economic point of view, be far wiser to leave the production of books to the likes of John Grisham and Stephen King—writers capable of attracting economically viable audiences—and to content myself with being a consumer of books, which I could well afford were I to undertake some commercially desirable form of labor. Is there any excuse, then, for persisting in my work?

This was the problem that Henry David Thoreau faced when he went to Walden Pond. He was, it seemed, unemployable, and the work to which he felt called paid no money. On what basis might he proceed with his life?

Had Thoreau lived in the late twentieth century, he might have applied for a mid-career development grant and taken a year off to upgrade his resumé, to cultivate his contacts with publishers, or to undertake a publicity tour of major eastern seaboard markets. Instead, he planted beans and asked himself what kind of life he desired and what might be necessary, in a material sense, to achieve it. Very little, he famously concluded: shelter from the elements, something to eat, and, as a concession to propriety, something to wear. The insight was antimaterialistic, but that was not its point. If you need things I myself can do without, Thoreau insisted, by all means seek to obtain them. You should not strive to live my life any more than you should live your mother's, your father's, or anyone else's; live *your* life. But do the math first, balancing the material books against the intangible ones.

Which, for example, would bring the greatest profit, all things considered: a can of store-bought tomatoes, a jar of home-preserved ones, or a paper entitled, "The True Cost of Home Food Preservation"?

While the water in blue kettle came to a boil, I washed the tomatoes. They were organically grown — not hydroponically perfect specimens from the market — and they were soiled, sometimes blemished, and not uniformly ripe, but they had all experienced direct contact with soil, sunshine, and rain and beneath their rather delicate skins they had absorbed the flavors of this experience. Tomatoes, like human beings, seem to benefit from being permitted to express their individuality.

In religious thought there have been two broad generalizations about human nature: either that we have sinned and fallen short of the glory of God, or that human beings are, at the core, good. Either belief provides a basis, when human relationships falter, for forgiveness, reconciliation, and reform, because both forbid claiming the high moral ground, from which the need for dominance may be served, but never the possibility of mutuality. In the absence of self-reflection, which the assumption of the high moral ground prevents, it is impossible either to sympathize with the fallibility of the other or to appeal to the other's innate goodness. There is no functional difference between self-loathing and other-loathing; in the first instance the other disappears, and in the second, the self does. A healthy relationship depends upon the presence of both the self and the other in each of the participants.

The community and the individual are not mutually exclusive; they are symbiotic. Just as constrictions of form enable creative expression, so the constraints of community stimulate individualism. Communities, by the same token, thrive on diversity; to the extent that communities suppress variablility they lose vitality. The more totalitarian a society is, the more severely it represses individuality. The freer it is, the more toleration it can afford.

Thoreau assailed materialism not because he wished to disavow things or ownership; he took immense pleasure, for example, in building his own house. And he celebrated individualism not because he disavowed community—he was, perhaps, bound to a fault to Concord and to his mother's house in it—but because he cherished freedom. He saw how materialism indentured his neighbors. A man with a mortgage, he thought, is to that extent a man fettered. And he saw how consensus limits moral action; it is possible, he thought, to honor a community by refusing, while one person acting alone, to participate in the evil it does

even while remaining loyal to it. He refused to pay a
Concord tax that indirectly supported slavery, but he
never considered, in protest, moving to Boston.

The notion that individualism threatens communities is rather like the notion that uniformity indicates
quality in tomatoes. It is an industrial idea, the strange
expectation that communities, like factories, can be built
to a standard of convenience.

I dropped the tomatoes into the boiling water, let them
simmer for a minute, and then plunged them into ice
water. When they were cool enough to handle, their
skins slipped off as easily as shirts, exposing flesh so vi-
brantly red that it might have been blushing. I trimmed
the stems, cut away the blemishes, and removed the
seeds from their chambers. Lying there on the cutting
board, red and many-chambered, they did look like
hearts.

My wife and I, married for more than a year, were
at her parents' house for dinner one Sunday evening.
The table talk often consisted of everybody declaiming
at once while I, earnest and insecure, the family's dis-
appointment, endeavored to be an attentive five-way
audience. The conversation, if one could call it that,
suddenly and uncharacteristically flagged between the
lamb roast and the blueberry pie.

In the lull, Jean Mary, my mother-in-law, turned
to me. "It's time that I had a name," she said in her
frank way. "We can't go on like this. What are you going
to call me?"

I had avoided the issue. Mrs. Harding seemed too
formal, Jean Mary too presumptuous, Mother too intimate. I had no other ideas.

I stammered, stared frantically at my plate, avoiding

her amused glaze. The iceberg lettuce and tomato salad came into sharp focus.

"I will call you Tomato," I said. I meant to deflect the question with a frivolity. I was innocent of the slang of her era.

She had a throaty bark of a laugh. It rang out across the dining room. "Oh thank you, dear," she said. She took a long, theatrical drag on her unfiltered Chesterfield, like a 1930s film star. She was, in her thin and angular way, striking, if not conventionally beautiful. She would have looked wonderful on film. The chatter resumed at a higher and jauntier pitch.

I had passed, apparently, some kind of test. I couldn't wait until we were in the car and on the way home again to ask Nancy what it was that I had actually said.

The chopped tomatoes nearly filled my biggest stockpot. I set it on the burner, brought the contents to a boil, and adjusted the heat to keep them at a steady simmer. The sweet, slightly acidic aroma of tomatoes began to fill the kitchen. There was nothing to do for the next hour but to stir the pot occasionally and to wait for the tomatoes, in the alchemy of heat, to give up their water and be reduced to their essence.

Beyond the kitchen windows the sunshine of early autumn bathed the last flowers of the season — chrysanthemums, New England asters, sedums, gentians — in a dissipating warmth. Fall is the season of distillation. One sees this process in the flowers, which deepen as they mature, eschewing the pallid whites and lavenders of spring, the sunny yellows and bawdy reds of summer, for deep hues of russet and bronze, purple and blue. There is, especially, no blue quite so intensely and purely blue as that of the gentians, the last prairie flowers of the year.

I would like my own life now to be like the color of autumn blossoms or these tomatoes slowly boiling down to their essence, I thought. I would like to be able to see my life clearly and directly, in its essential lines, like those drawings of Matisse's that I admired once at the Minneapolis Institute of Arts: a line here and one there, six or eight to a page, the simplest possible strokes of a pencil out of which emerged the whole complexity of human emotion and experience.

When the chunks of tomato in the stockpot had lost their form and the emerging sauce had begun to thicken, I filled the big blue canning kettle with water and set it to boil. It was time to sterilize the jars and lids. The kitchen, as the second pot came to boil, filled with steam. The sounds of tomatoes burbling in their pot and the kettle of sterilizing water pinging on its burner, the steam rising on the desultory afternoon air, and the intimacy of the gathering heat all reminded me of mornings long ago: Father in the garden picking produce by the milk pailful; my sisters, my grandparents, and I at a table in the yard shelling peas, stringing beans, shucking corn, hulling ground cherries; and Mother in the kitchen, a scarf tied around her brow to catch the sweat, tending the alarming pressure cookers that she used for canning, watching the pressure gauges and the timers closely, lest too much steam build up and the cookers blow their covers, and at the same time deftly retrieving sterile jars from their hot-water bath, filling them with produce, screwing down the caps tightly over their lids, setting recently processed jars out to cool, and, just at the right moment, when a new batch of jars had been processed long enough, pulling the cookers off the fire, throwing open their steamcocks, and leaping back out of the way of the plumes of steam that shot up like geysers.

There was a faint air of danger and of frenzy those mornings, something acrobatic and graceful about my mother in the canning kitchen. It was a challenge to which she rose with an awesome poise quite unlike her everyday demeanor.

We children were not permitted for a long time to see this side of her. Once, when we were still very small, my sister stole into the kitchen while Mother was filling jars with boiling apple butter, grabbed her from behind, and shouted "Boo!" Mother, who had been oblivious to everything but her work, started and spilled the boiling butter onto my giggling sister's bare arms. After that, for many years, we were banned from the canning kitchen. Not until we were in our teens were we permitted to watch Mother again at her dexterous and masterful work.

The labor went on all summer. By fall, when the potatoes were finally tucked away in their earthen bins and the late apples had been individually wrapped in sheets of newsprint and packed in tin barrels, the cellar shelves would be laden with more than 700 jars of produce: fruits and savory sauces, potted meats, pickles and relishes, jellies and jams, marmalades and butters, vegetables and vegetable juices.

Tucked away in a corner all their own were the show jars, the ones painstakingly packed at the peak of the season with the most perfect and handsome specimens of the crop: the longest and lithest string beans arranged in spirals; the choicest cucumbers, standing erect in their clarified brine; the reddest tomatoes; the tiniest beets, swimming in blood-colored broths; the strained jellies, shimmering beneath their parafin caps, each stamped with an heirloom seal. For each commodity, there was a special batch of six jars, from which a final selection would be made, after close scrutiny in a strong morning light, for showing at the county and state fairs. They won many ribbons, mostly purples and blues, with rewards of a dollar or two apiece. The money went into the common kitty, the ribbons—for the same reason, I suppose, that no farmer in our neighborhood ever publically admitted to having harvested a good crop—were hidden away in some obscure box and ultimately lost. But there was no hiding the pride that mother took in being a champion canner.

Until I sat thinking about her in my own kitchen that Saturday, I would have said that my mother was a plain country woman with few ambitions, but I realize now how wrong that perception was. When she was not canning, she baked her wonderful bread, or wove rugs from scraps of discarded clothing, or made crazywork quilts, or brewed wines that, given the abstemious tenor of our household, were not intended for drinking—a shotglass of the wine per adult on Christmas Eve constituted our annual consumption of alcohol, although it was, I learned when I myself became an adult, a shot that packed a considerable wallop—or sewed elaborate wedding and christening gowns and prom formals on consignment, or made the clothes that we ourselves wore. Scarcely a day of her life passed in which she did not create something intended to be beautiful or delectable as well as practical.

Because she was a farmwoman, her labors could be dismissed as the drudging lot of poor rural women everywhere, but I realize now that she was, after all, an artist of dedication and accomplishment. Her own mother left behind two yard-square needlepoint tapestries depicting scenes from her Norwegian childhood. One was begun in 1930 and finished in 1935. The other, begun in 1936, was finished in 1940. Each required hundreds of thousands, perhaps millions, of tiny, precise stitches, made on winter evenings by kerosene light by guidance of a pair of images she kept in her head. One might call them pieces of folk art, except that they are not crude or naive in any way. They are like pointillist paintings in which the individual and many-colored stiches, from a certain distance, miraculously come together in scenes of astonishing realism and depth: needlepoint masterpieces. My great-grandmother, whom I never met, achieved such mastery, too. In the linen drawer opposite the pantry I have a lace tablecloth tatted by her, a piece of such elegance that I dare not use it, for fear of defiling it with a careless stain.

I have come, although I did not realize it until I set out one Saturday to preserve a batch of tomatoes, from a long line of artists.

To remember their work in this way might be dismissed as nostalgic, but it is *not* nostalgic. These women, my mother, my grandmother, my great-grandmother, experienced the ordinary burdens of pain and sorrow, suffered the standard lot of tedium and toil, went to their graves with the customary number of regrets and recriminations, and sinned in all the usual ways. Their lives may have been bittersweet, but they were not unsweetened, and that, as any baker knows, makes all the difference.

One night in midwinter we were awakened by the sound of a powerful but muffled explosion. It sounded as if the house were falling in. Father got up and made a tour of the premises. Everything seemed in order. He went back to bed, we fell back to sleep again, and the night passed uneventfully.

The next afternoon I went to the cellar through the exterior trapdoor to fetch a jar of string beans and one of tomatoes for the barley chowder that my mother was making, her best supper dish. When I switched on the light, I saw that the row of shelves along the back wall of the cellar had collapsed. The cellar floor was strewn with the rubble of hundreds of shattered jars. Their contents had seeped into every corner of the room and the air was ripe with the smell of garlic and onions, dill and vinegar.

I ran to the kitchen to tell Mother what had happened. She looked ashen. "Go get your father," she said, her voice strangely soft and deflated.

I found him in the barn milking the goats. He finished with the last of the nannies. We walked across the yard, our boots crunching in the snow. I did not dare look at him. When we got to the front door, he handed me the pail of steaming milk. "Go on in with this and help your mother," he said gently. I went in, not knowing what I might do to be helpful. Mother sat at the kitchen table with her head in her hands. I sat beside her. Below in the cellar we could hear the clank and tinkle of glass and the scraping of a shovel. The noise went on for a long time. Then there was silence, and the front door opened. "I need the broom," he said. He was holding a jar of tomatoes and one of string beans in his hands.

Mother got the broom and took the jars. She went to the stove and finished her chowder. It was the same excellent chowder she always made.

When she brought it to the table, Father said the same prayer he aways said. "Bless us and these, thy gifts, which thou has made. In Jesus' name, amen." We ate in silence, the sound of our spoons clicking against the bowls.

When the meal was finished, Father looked at Mother and grinned. She seemed about to cry, but what came from her throat was a giggle, then both of them laughed outright, and when the tears finally came, it was impossible to tell what part of her heart was crying.

With a pair of tongs, I fished the hot pints, lids, and rings out of the canning kettle and set them in a row on the counter. Into each jar I ladeled some of the thick sauce, to which I had added a bit of salt and just enough vinegar to conserve the color, nothing more. This sauce would be a statement against decadence, celebrating the elegant essence of tomatoes, a complexity unneedful of elaboration.

I lowered the jars into the boiling water and bathed them for ten minutes, brought them up again into the late afternoon air, gave the rings one more twist to ensure that the lids would seal, set them out to cool, and started another batch.

It was early evening when the last of the jars was finished. The quiet of dusk in the incadescent light of my kitchen was punctuated by the hollow pop of jar lids being drawn down into airtight vacuum seals.

When the jars were cool enough to handle, I found myself doing something I remembered my mother doing at the end of a day of canning. I removed the rings from the jars and put them away in a box for another time, and then, with a wet cloth and a towel at hand, I took up each jar in turn, polished it, held it up against the light to admire it, and set it carefully aside. When all the jars were sparkling in a row, I sat in a chair at the kitchen table, feeling pleasantly weary, and admired them some more from a little distance, the rosy summation of a good day's work.

# Bones

I HAVE ALWAYS had an eye for bones. As a child, I collected and arranged them by size on a hayloft shelf in the barn. On rainy summer afternoons and snowy winter days, I retired to my museum to play with the bones, turning them over in my hands, examining them in the dim light seeping through the cracks in the barn walls, running my fingers over worn incisors, feeling the bald smoothness of skull bones, admiring the way femurs balanced in my hands, listening to the wind in the cupolas and to the cooing of pigeons, hearing raindrops or ice crystals shattering against the shingles. The bones spoke to me on those dank afternoons, but I was a long time in deciphering what they said.

From the beginning there were some bones I declined to collect. In the sinkhole at the bottom of our pasture a cow had mired and died, years before I chanced upon it. The flesh had rotted away long before, devoured by billions of microbes. Nothing remained but a few tufts of brown hair, some scraps of leathery hide, and the bones. Bleached and graying, they lay half buried in the muck, contorted still in the last paroxysm of life. The cow's skull had separated from the upper vertebrae and rested upwind from the rest of its skeleton, facing north into the bitter winds.

I first encountered these remains one cold November afternoon when the leaves had fallen from the willows and the sedges had turned russet and golden. A pheasant bolted from the meadow grasses underfoot, startling me, and when I looked down, I was staring into the vacant sockets where the cow's eyes had been. The skull seemed to be staring back at me.

My first impulse was to collect the bones of the mired cow, but I resisted. Some integrity in them restrained me. Everything else in my collection had appeared at random: a skull here, a rib cage there, leavings scattered by scavengers, by wind, water, and frost. To pick up such a bone is to become part of its natural history, to join the forces of dispersal at restless work in the world. But the bones of the cow, for whatever reasons, had remained intact, held in the continuing entrapment of the sinkhole. The site harbored something more than a death. It seemed to me that the cow was entombed there, and my passion for bones did not extend to the robbery of graves.

I was only a boy, but I knew something of graves. I knew the scent of gladiolas and strong perfume that hung in Grandfather's parlor, where his embalmed body had been displayed for viewing before the ritual of the grave. I had felt the strong, icy wind blowing across the open prairie cemetery on the brown day when they buried him and the cold clank of a pebble hurled upon the burnished bronze casket with the first shovel of earth. I remembered, even then, nothing of my living grandfather, but the memory of his bones lingers still. And I knew the smell of urine and rubber in the sickroom of my grandmother, the same parlor that had held my dead grandfather. She had been laid out there in a rented hospital bed to die, insensible after a stroke. We watched as she shriveled day by day into a sack of sharp-edged bones.

I had dug my share of graves. I made one for the cottontail rabbit I had been raising in a chicken-wire cage in the backyard. I found it abandoned as an infant and had tended it all summer, feeding it with an eye-dropper until it could be weaned. I brought it fresh tidbits from the garden, young cabbages and carrots and leaves of lettuce, treating it as the younger brother I did not have.

"You have got to let that rabbit go," my father had been saying. "The sooner the better. It can't stay the winter in that pen. It won't survive."

"Yes," I said, "I'll do it. Tomorrow."

One admonishment led to another, one tomorrow into the next. There were many distractions, and I didn't want to relinquish the rabbit.

One morning late in September, I went out, bare-footed and still in my pajamas, to feed it, and found the rabbit quivering in a corner of its box, bleeding thickly from several savage gashes inflicted by some predator. I wept as I treated the rabbit's wounds, but it did not survive the day. In the evening I buried the corpse in the grove, my heart heavier for the conviction, vain no doubt, that had the rabbit not been penned it might have escaped. At that age, I still had faith in a benign and brotherly nature and felt personally betrayed when that nature spoke to me in the language of violence and death.

On another day, a hot one in July, I learned to speak the same language myself. I had a cat, for whom I had vowed responsibility, that had produced a litter of kittens. I could not keep them, I had been emphatically told, and, as desperately as I tried, I could find no one else to adopt them. None of the farming folks I knew needed or wanted another cat. So one awful day, in a terrible heat, I took them into an abandoned henhouse to do what needed to be done. One by one I picked up the lovely, mewing kittens and held them at the bottom of a bucket of water. When they stopped struggling, I carried them into the grove where the rabbit's bones rested, made ten tiny graves, and buried them like pieces of my own flesh. I hated my own flesh then, hated the ruthless efficiency with which it could be made to do such dirty work, and would as soon have buried myself. But another part of me yearned to live as violently as had those kittens when they were suffocating in a water pail in the close heat of a July afternoon.

There were many kinds of bones in those days: the leg bone our big tomcat chewed off when it had been snapped in a trap and had withered and rotted; the bones, stinking like old tires burning, of the family goats,

caught in a fire I had carelessly set; the neck bones of
chickens crunching under the blows of my ax on
butchering days; the carcasses of the rodents I had
trapped, skinned, and offered to my dog, Mitsy, as a sac-
rifice of love; the bones of the ground squirrels I
drowned in their holes and sold to the county government for a bounty of ten cents a head; the bones I
carried home from my wanderings in fields and meadows. These days I live a more genteel life, one that has
little to do with bones and one a lot farther from nature.

The bones often told cruel stories, some of them of
my own creation. What was I supposed to make of this?
The obvious thing, that life is sometimes cruel, I suppose. It is a fact more to be respected than explained,
like the fact that when you try your tongue on the pump
handle in the wintertime, it bonds to the metal and you
cannot pry it lose without tearing away some skin. I
couldn't explain cruelty, and I didn't try. When my father
insisted that my sister wear skirts to the school bus stop
half a mile away in vicious midwinter because he had religious scruples against allowing females to wear trousers,
and when she froze her legs and whimpered all the way
to school from the sting and itch of the thawing, I
thought him cruel and stupid and pious to a horrible
fault, but I still loved him, and so, in her own way, did
she. Our love was a mystery, but when was life or love
ever not a mystery?

I vowed at a fairly early age to try to give up volun-
tary cruelties, stopped keeping wild pets, quit hunting
and trapping for sport. I practiced a boyish and irregular
asceticism, finding myself, although Protestant, power-
fully attracted for a time to the most extravagant habits
of the third- and fourth-century desert eremites. One
saint, whose name I've forgotten, particularly enchanted

me. I read that he had spent forty days and forty nights sitting motionless in a swamp, enduring impassively whatever abuses came his way, in penance for having swatted a mosquito, one of God's creatures. I did not dare to hope for such saintliness, but I did, for a time, passionately admire it.

Still, I remained a cruel person. In the winter I ate the sheep that had pulled me around the yard in a cart in the summertime, feeling neither gratitude nor regret. I fished for northerns in the rapids below the dam on the river, not for food but for the fun of it. For some grim reason, I particularly enjoyed beheading grasshoppers and spent many pleasant hours doing so in the grain wagons at harvest time. It was a crooked world, running along an ambiguous path overgrown with many obstructions, and I could not see the straight way through it.

I suffer over this with my own children. Once, as we were sitting around a campfire, I absentmindedly crushed a cricket that had crawled near the flame. My daughter burst into tears. I did not know what she was crying about, which made everything much worse. I begged her to explain what was wrong.

"You murdered it!" she finally said, between her sobs.

"Murdered it! Murdered what?" I said.

She stopped crying, looked at me coldly. "I suppose you really don't know," she said.

I looked blank.

"The cricket!" she said. "The poor helpless cricket! Why did you have to go and do that? It wasn't hurting anything, was it?"

"No," I had to admit, "it wasn't."

At the same time, I was impatient and unrepenting. My God, I thought, I once aspired to an eremitic sensibility, and now I have raised one. "Be reasonable," I wanted to say. And, "You know, there are greater tragedies in life than the wanton death of a cricket." But I kept silent, out of confusion and embarrassment, and because I did not want to endorse wantonness, however trivial. I understood that in a moral sense she was right. One of the troubles with morality is its indifference to distinctions of degree, its impracticality.

My son, at that age, on the other hand, saw nature as many children do, as something to pillage, to plunder, to maim, to shoot, or to catch. Every wild creature was meant, so far as he was concerned, to be carried home on a stringer or carted home in a box or glass bottle.

One night on a camping trip we fished for bull-heads, a sport in which I indulge him, although I do not enjoy it myself. I dislike it out of contempt: for the ease with which bullheads may be caught, for the execrable waters they inhabit, for their slimy skins that seem to get slimier as the summer wears on, for the greedy way they swallow hooks, for the grotesque belches they emit when you squeeze their air bladders, as you must if you wish to avoid their painful barns when unhooking them. I suspect all hierarchies, but there is no doubt in my mind that any one bass or trout or walleye is infinitely more desirable than any dumpster full of bullheads.

That day we caught a mess of bullheads, and because the two of us were on an indulgent father-and-son outing, I agreed to let him carry them back to camp — actually, after a few yards, I carried them myself — and promised to cook them for breakfast. We stashed the fish in the minnow bucket, watched the fire burn down and the heavens come alive, and went to bed. An hour or two later, I was awakened by the clatter of dishes. Peering into the moonlit night, I saw a raccoon sitting next to the opened camping box on the picnic table, picking marsh-mallows daintily out of a bag and eating them one at a time, very noisily and with much smacking of lips.

A raccoon is an exceedingly handsome and beguiling creature. I rather regretted getting up out of habit and shooing it away. I stashed the marshmallows in the car and went back to bed. Fifteen minutes later the animal was back. This time it took hold of the minnow bucket, dragged it a little way off, tipped it on its side, inserted one paw through its trapdoor to hold it open, fished one bullhead at a time out of the bucket, and ate them, smacking its lips even more loudly. It was clear from the aplomb with which it executed this banquet that the raccoon was an old veteran of the minnow-bucket circuit.

Delighted, I made no attempt to stop it. The raccoon's gain was all the more mine. In my mind I substituted pancakes for bullheads at breakfast and went contentedly, even joyfully, to sleep. In the morning I put on a sad face and confessed the tragedy to my son. I expected him to be heartbroken, but he wasn't in the least. He has always been an optimist, and he immediately saw a grander opportunity.

"I know what!" he said. "Let's go catch some more bullheads, and then we can use them for bait and catch that old raccoon!"

"But why would you want to do that?" I said, and then, looking into his face and seeing the futility in such a question, I lied. "We'll see," I said.

I want to find some middle ground between the naive reverence of my daughter and the nature-as-sport attitude of my son. Once, I think, I had found it, but as my life grew more complicated, I lost it. I am thinking of that brief time when I was a country boy and lived in the out-of-doors essentially as one might occupy a living room. I didn't make the distinctions then that I routinely do now, because the distinctions between inside and outside, between wild and domestic, between house and home, did not, for practical purposes, exist.

I was never confined as a child in Chippewa County, Minnesota, to any space so constricted as a house. Of course our family had a house, or a succession of them, that I shared: first a cement-block basement house, then a balloon-frame shack, finally an honest, full-fledged farmhouse with rooms and staircases and a real basement and rag rugs on the linoleum floors. But none of these houses fully contained the place where I lived. In the country one lives not in a house but on a farm and thinks of the space one occupies as including everything within its fence lines. But for me, something more was at work. In our little country church I heard often the promise of heaven. I visualized it not as cloudy and ethereal but as a concrete place, according to the words of Jesus: "In my father's house are many mansions." I thought of my own Minnesota home as a smaller version of heaven, as a house of many mansions. There was the wooden-frame house with the green mansard roof where I slept and ate and joined the life of the family. But it was only one of my many mansions.

I lived, for one thing, in the hayloft where I stored my collection of bones. When it was too stormy to be outside, I was likely to spend the day there, swinging from the ropes or standing in the crow's nest at the peak of the gables where I could see out across the river valley through a little round window. I kept company with the pigeons, read, napped in a bed of hay, teased spiders out of their chambers, daydreamed.

And I lived with squirrels and pale tree frogs in the limbs of an enormous black walnut tree at the far end of the pasture. It was always shady there, and a fresh breeze always seemed, even in the stillest and hottest weather, to be blowing around that tree. Its limbs were broad enough to lie down upon, as I often did, listening to the murmur of summer afternoons, the buzzing of flies, the droning of bumblebees, the singing of birds. Near it were the hollow of a pioneer's sod hut and a sweet-water spring that ran all winter. I imagined that the sod house was mine in the making, that the spring had drawn me there, and that I would live forever in the shadow of the wide arms of the walnut tree.

I lived also along the shores of the pasture pond, where the pussy willows swelled in the springtime; and blackbirds wheezed and wheedled in the cattails; and muskrats swam in the musty, warm summer waters, green with algae and duckweed. I lived among the arrowroots and jewelweeds, among the strawberries hiding in the cordgrass, among minks, weasels, and fat skunks. Water striders and boatmen and pill bugs squatted in my front yard, right-handed pond snails and leopard frogs in my backyard, dragonflies and damselflies in the fetid air overhead. I passed many happy hours in the upper reaches of a black willow tree, monitoring the progress of life in the fecund chambers of my pond mansion.

And I lived by the blue light of the moon along country lanes so quiet I could hear the town traffic miles away, visible only as a burst of mysterious light on the distant horizon. Fireflies flashed in the road ditches, and long leaves of corn sighed in the evening breezes. Here and there a dog barked in a farmyard. The sound of dogs barking in the night, of their barks echoing across the vast, empty countryside, was the surfacing sound of

the wildness in them. I could hear in their voices the ancient cries of gray wolves in the days when great herds of
bison roamed the plains and the moonlight danced in
the endless waves of grass. I could feel then the wildness
in my own bones.

And I lived in a woodpile, in a plum thicket, in the
striped shade of an August cornfield, where the whirligigs
raced across the sweltering landscape, showering dust like
rain. And in a prairie meadow, among overgrazed river
bluffs, on a granite island in a widening of the river, along
a grassy fenceline where a lone green ash grew.

Again, I lived along the riverbanks where beaver
built their dams; mud turtles sunned on half-submerged
logs; bullheads and northern pike, saugers and buffalo
fish swam the murky waters; white-tailed deer came down
to drink; the tracks of mink mingled in the shoreline
mud with the remains of the deer-toe clams they had
fished from the shallows.

But mainly I dwelled along the river under the spell
of its mysterious waters, which ran to the Minnesota
River, then into the Mississippi River, then down the central nervous cord of the continent, over the plains of
Iowa, through the hills of Missouri and Arkansas, across
the bayous of Louisiana, and into the Gulf of Mexico.

In my house there were many mansions.

When I sat on the overhanging limb of a willow tree
dangling my bare feet into the brown Chippewa River,
feeling the slow, steady tug of its unfailing current
against my toes, I became connected to the great body of
the continent. I was linked not merely with a small river
in western Minnesota but swept up into the gigantic
stream of life. I lived then in the piney waters of the
North Woods, in the thundering waters of St. Anthony
Falls, in the icy rush of mountain streams, in the stagnant

backwaters of southern marshes, in the oceanic brine. I shared then a mansion with my little bullheads, yes, but also with ancient paddlefishes and cutthroat trout and sharks and catfishes as big as logs. I lived then among bald eagles and alligators and panthers. I lived where it always snows and where it never snows, high in the mountains and at the edge of the sea.

As a high school biology student, I once traced the cardiovascular system of a domestic cat whose blood vessels had been injected with a rubbery substance, blue for the veins, red for the arteries. Beginning at the heart, I traced the vessels up into its skull and down into its toes and out along its tail, following them as they branched into smaller and smaller streams. It was an ecstatic experience; I carried my half-excavated specimen home in a clear plastic bag, unable to bear the suspense of waiting until the next day's class to discover where all the vessels ran. No one would sit in the same bus seat with me, but I was too excited to mind. There in the body of the cat lay a map of the world as I perceived it from my vantage point along the Chippewa River. I might be one tiny red corpuscle swimming in the slenderest of the tail arteries, but I was an undeniable part of something big and alive, a constituent particle of the whole organism. I had seen the universe in a two-dollar laboratory specimen.

Now I live in a single house of eight rooms, from which I venture forth into nature as a tourist. Most mornings I walk from my house around a shallow prairie lake to the two-room office in which I spend my days pacing, writing, reading, staring out of the second-story windows into the canopy of a black walnut tree. It buds, it leafs, it flowers, it bears nuts. The yellow-green nuts turn brown and fall; the green leaves to yellow and flutter to earth.

In the winter I watch frozen pieces of the tree break off
in the wind and scatter to the earth. In the spring the
tree buds again. Some would call this a cycle, the eternal
cycle of nature, and find comfort in it, but I don't. Every
spring the tree is a little older, and so am I. The progres-
sion, so far as the individual is concerned, whether it be
a tree or me, is linear: it ends in death every time. The
best that can be said, in the meantime, is that neither of
us has moved.

The skies beyond the tree change. One day dawns
clear, the next cloudy. Some days rain patters against the
window glass. Some mornings the branches of the walnut
tree are white with rime frost, others with new snow. The
wind blows, or doesn't. In the heated and air-condi-
tioned solitude of my study, it is all the same.

One summer afternoon a year or two ago the sky
suddenly turned as black as ink. The streetlights switched
on. A stillness fell, so deafening as to intrude even into
my already silent rooms. Rain began to pour in a torrent
as it does in the rain forest on tropical afternoons. The
downpour was swept and swirled by violent winds that
howled in the corners of the building. As suddenly as the
rain came, so came the hail, thundering down upon the
rooftop and smashing against the windows. One by one
the panes of glass shattered while I cowered in the middle of the outer room, paralyzed with awe and fear.
Then, as suddenly as it arrived, the storm passed. The
branches of the walnut tree hung in tatters, icy water
puddled on the sills of the jagged, broken windows, and
in the streets mist had already begun to rise from the
drifts of ice dissipating in the sun. Ten million dollars
worth of damage in ten minutes in one small prairie
town. I thought of a classroom outburst of John
Berryman's on another summer day when I was a student

of his. Suddenly, on the way to the lectern to deliver a lecture on James Joyce, he had smashed a chair into the orchestra pit and bellowed incoherently against janitors. "It was good for them," he later wrote of us, his bewildered students. "A Zen touch:/ action in the midst of thought."

But most days are not graced with such drama. They come quietly to a close and I walk home, noticing, perhaps, whether it is hot or cold, windy or calm, passing through a landscape so familiar that I have ceased to see it, and ready to take up residence for the night in the only house I now know, a gray one of eight rooms, a tight fortress against the world beyond its windows. I take the telephone off the hook, throw the junk mail unopened in the wastebasket, and sit in my brown chair in the yellow light of a lamp listening to someone's arrangement of piano music on a compact disc. There are rooms in the house that I seldom visit, and, so far as I am concerned, there are no other houses anywhere else in the wide world.

When I want, these days, to visit the mansions in which I once lived, I pack the car, arrange my schedule, consult maps, visit the local stores for perishable supplies, and set out from my house as a tourist, fearful sometimes, but full of new energy, too, as one always is at the beginning of a journey. And when I arrive and set out on foot into some untamed place, I come sooner or later to a bone or a shell. I keep such souvenirs here in my office or on the fireplace mantel in my house: the tooth of a bison washed out of the mud of a Nebraska streambed; the carapace of a horseshoe crab picked up in a Florida mangrove swamp; a bowl of fossil teeth collected on a Gulf of Mexico beach; the shell of a land snail found in

the sandy soil of an arroyo in the Baja desert; the jaw-
bone of a cow from the Great Basin of Wyoming; the
scales of an ancient gar fish found eroding out of the soft
stone of the North Dakota Badlands; the skull of a mule
deer attacked by coyotes on Montana's Front Range.
Every bone reminds me of many others that I left uncol-
lected somewhere. Like the prophet, I have walked in a
valley full of bones.

The remarkable thing, in fact, is that one finds so
few bones. Millions of creatures die every day. Where are
their remains? Where have they all gone? And as for the
dying creatures, where are they? You can walk for a thousand miles and never once see a creature dying. Death is
nothing if not discrete.

The bones, every one, are miracles, the alms nature
offers to life. It is hard to believe in miracles. They seem
to fall beyond the boundaries of cause and effect. But a
miracle is nothing more than a story that begins after the
event. It is the mysterious space between the particles of
a story, like the space between the particles of an atom,
that makes the substance of things possible. The miracle
of a bone is that it is the evidence of something particular that once lived, something unprecedented, and
never to be repeated, that has vanished yet nevertheless
endures in bone, a faint white glimmering, in some
offhand place, of life everlasting.

# Notes

Portions of this book have previously appeared as follows:

Portions of "Home Is a Place in Time" (Autumn 1993) and "The Transfiguration of Bread" (Spring 1994) were first published in *Connections*, the newsletter of The Minnesota Project.

Parts of "Rosewood Township" first appeared in *Townships;* ed. Michael Martone (Ames: Iowa State University Press, 1990).

"Remember the Flowers" was first published with the title "An Excellent Life" in *Minnesota Monthly* (May 1987); as were "Snails Have Faces," with the title "The Task of Discovery" (August 1988); "Dreaming in West Bend, Iowa," with the title "Redemption" (November 1988); and "Bones" (July 1988), which was reprinted in *The Best American Essays, 1989*.

"What the Prairie Teaches Us" first appeared in (February 1991) *Cooperative Partners*, the Cenex/Land O'Lakes customer magazine.

"What We Teach Rural Children" was first presented as a lecture at St. Mary's College, Winona, Minnesota, October 17, 1990.

"Guerilla Warfare to Revive the Countryside" was first a talk for a gathering of the Winona Diocese of the Catholic Church, March 30, 1993.

"What Time Is It?" was a talk to the members of the Cannon River Watershed Partnership, April 3, 1993.

"Visions" took form as a lecture to the Minnesota Academy of Ophthamology, January 13, 1995.

The following material is quoted in this book:

The Thoreau quotations are all from *Walden* (New York: Library of America, 1985): "None is so poor that he need sit on a pumpkin," p. 374; "I went to the woods because I wanted to live deliberately . . . ," p. 394; "I learned this, at least, by my experiment . . . ," p. 580; "Superfluous wealth can buy superfluities only. . . . ," p. 584.

*The Unsettling of America: Culture and Agriculture* is the title of a book by Wendell Berry (San Francisco: Sierra Club Books, 1977). The lines from Berry's poetry are from *Cleaving* (San Diego: Harcourt Brace Jovanovich, 1974), p. 19.

The crowd statistic on p. 96 was provided by the Worthington, Minnesota, Chamber of Commerce. The estimate of remaining tallgrass prairie comes from the Nature Conservancy.

The Hudson quotation is from *Plains Country Towns* by John C. Hudson (Minneapolis: University of Minnesota Press, 1985), p. 148.

PAUL GRUCHOW is a freelance writer and farm owner living in Northfield, Minnesota. He has authored four previous books, including *Journal of a Prairie Year* (University of Minnesota Press, 1985) and *The Necessity of Empty Places* (St. Martin's Press, 1988), and published hundreds of articles, essays, and reviews in periodicals such as *Nature Conservancy, The Hungry Mind Review,* and *The Utne Reader.* He has been an assistant professor of English and is a frequent lecturer and speaker on rural issues and literature.

Cover designed by Adrian Morgan
Cover photo by Michael Melford, Inc.
Interior designed by Will Powers
Typeset in Baskerville and Insignia
by Stanton Publication Services, Inc.
Printed on acid-free 55# Booktext Natural paper
by BookCrafters.

More essays from Milkweed Editions:

*Bad Government and Silly Literature*
Carol Bly

*The Passionate, Accurate Story*
*Making Your Heart's Truth into Literature*
Carol Bly

*The Art of Writing*
*Lu Chi's Wen Fu*
Translated from the Chinese
by Sam Hamill

*Rooms in the House of Stone*
Michael Dorris

*The Mythic Family*
Judith Guest

*Coming Home Crazy*
*An Alphabet of China Essays*
Bill Holm

*I Won't Learn from You!*
*The Role of Assent in Learning*
Herbert Kohl

*A Male Grief*
*Notes on Pornography and Addiction*
David Mura

*Homestead*
Annick Smith

*What Makes Pornography "Sexy"?*
John Stoltenberg

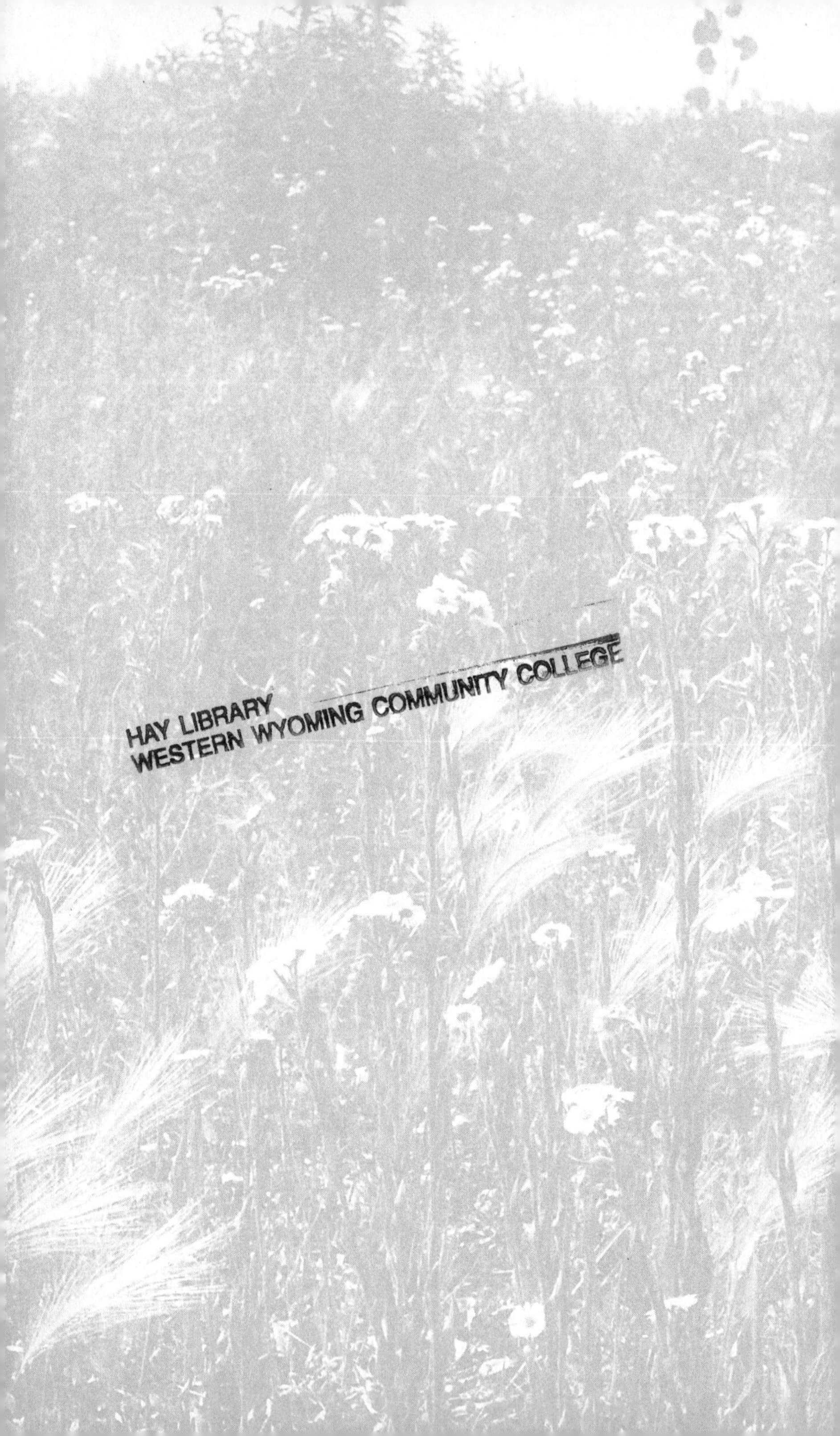